# THE Family Life Cookbook

# Index

**almonds**
activated almond milk 38
almond butter 71
almond-crusted chicken nuggets 282
**apple** 115
avocado apple smoothie 116
beetroot and apple juice 138
easy apple muffins 116
mini apple tarts 118
**asparagus**
pizza verde on cauliflower crust 168
**avocado** 271
avocado apple smoothie 116
avocado lime cheesecake 274
avocado smoothie pops 276
chocolate avocado muffins 272
green smoothie bowl 36
stop and go tortillas 24
**banana** 45
banana yoghurt popsicles 40
easy banana nut muffins 46
everyday banana loaf 146
green smoothie bowl 36
sticky sweet bananas 44
waffles with fresh fruit and nuts 52
**barbecue sauce** 166
**beans**
black bean, corn and quinoa salad 182
minestrone soup 212
**beef**
beef empanadas 226
bolognese bake 106
chilli con carne with cheese 180
meatballs in tomato sauce 246
mini cheeseburgers 288
shepherd's pie 244
**beetroot** 139
beetroot and apple juice 138
beetroot burgers 250
easy beetroot brownie 152
healthy beet balls 138
home-made veggie chips 89
**blueberries**
blueberry cake 130
butterfly puffs 292
cheat's berry ice cream 135
yoghurt berry cereal pops 135
**breadcrumbs** 281
**broccoli**
broccoli cheese sticks 246

**buckwheat**
buckwheat flour 49
buckwheat pancakes 44
**butter**
garden cupcakes 292
halloween witches' hats 298
princess cupcakes 256
real English scones 60
**cacao** 151
**carrot**
carrot risotto 188
carrot soup 218
crunchy carrot sushi 72
honey roast vegetables and crispy potatoes 204
minestrone soup 212
**cauliflower**
cauliflower hash browns 54
pizza verde on cauliflower crust 168
**cheese**
bolognese bake 106
broccoli cheese sticks 246
chedder and leek mini quiches 102
chilli con carne with cheese 180
cottage cheese pancakes 98
Mexican enchilada 176
mini cheeseburgers 288
pizza rolls 104
savoury muffins 28
**chia** 33
easy banana nut muffins 46
overnight raspberry chia pots 34
**chicken**
almond-crusted chicken nuggets 282
chicken lasagne 240
chicken pasta soup 218
chicken pumpkin kebab 164
chicken wontons 232
country-style chicken pie 224
easy tandoori chicken wraps 76
grilled chicken sesame kebabs with sesame sauce 162
home-made gravy 201
Mexican enchilada 176
miso chicken rolls 70
roast chicken with pan gravy 201
sticky chicken drumsticks 202

**chilli**
chilli con carne with cheese 180
sweet chilli sauce 166
**chocolate**
banana yoghurt popsicles 40
chocolate avocado muffins 272
chocolate fudge and white chocolate cake pops 268
easy beetroot brownie 152
energy balls 144
flourless chocolate muffins 84
homemade ice-cream sandwiches 260
mint choc chip blocks 276
spiced choc 'n' nut slice 154
**cinnamon** 117
**coconut**
coconut rice 186
mango and coconut balls 140
mango coconut slice 122
**corn**
black bean, corn and quinoa salad 182
**cottage cheese** 99
cottage cheese pancakes 98
**cucumber**
little cucumber people 296
**dried fruit**
spiced choc 'n' nut slice 154
**dumplings** 231, *see also dumpling ingredients*
**eggs** 17–18
baked egg and ham cups 20
gourmet ham and egg bagels 22
mini breakfast pizzas 26
mushroom tartlets 90
spider eggs 294
stop and go tortillas 24
the perfect boiled egg 26
**fish**
baked fish in crunchy breadcrumbs 194
fish cakes 242
fish tacos with mango salsa 178
takeaway fish and chips 170
**flaxseed** 33
hulk balls 142
**flours, gluten free** 49
**ginger**
gingerbread imagination cookies 258
**ham**
baked egg and ham cups 20
gourmet ham and egg bagels 22
pizza rolls 104

**HERRON**
book distributors

First Published in 2017 by Herron Book Distributors Pty Ltd
14 Manton St
Morningside
QLD 4170
www.herronbooks.com

Custom book production by Captain Honey Pty Ltd
PO Box 155
Byron Bay
NSW 2481
www.captainhoney.com.au

Cataloguing-in-Publication. A catalogue record for this book is available from the National Library of Australia

ISBN 978-0-947163-46-4

Printed and bound in China by Shenzhen Jinhao Color Printing Co., Ltd

5 4 3 2 1    17 18 19 20 21

## NOTES FOR THE READER

All reasonable efforts have been made to ensure the accuracy of the content in this book. Information in this book is not intended as a substitute for medical advice. The author and publisher cannot and do not accept any legal duty of care or responsibility in relation to the content in this book, and disclaim any liabilities relating to its use.

## PHOTO CREDITS

Front cover: marcin jucha
Back cover: Goskova Tatiana
3523studio p 77. aboikis p 208. avs p 238. Anastasia_Panait p 2. AS Food studio p 229. Agnes Kantaruk p 293. ArtCookStudio p 75. Africa Studio p 78. Aris Setya p 138. Anna_Pustynnikova p 277. Aleksandra Witkowska p 136. Amallia Eka p 143. Anna Mente p 128. Alliance p 300. Amawasri Pakdara p 39. Anastasia_Panait p 92, 160, 290. Alphonsine Sabine p 62. Anastasiia Markus p 156. Alinute Silzeviciute p 14. AnnaKurzaeva p 51. AS Food studio p 177, 218, 225, 266.Africa Studio p 59. Anna Shepulova p 197. Anna-Mari West p 135. Anna Mente p 37. alisafarov.jpg OK 215. Brent Hofacker p 183, 262, 227. Bonchan p 289. BravissimoS p 206. best-photo-studio p 158. Baibaz p 48. Brittny p 119. Bigacis p 150. baibaz p 59. beta7 p 87. BlueOrange Studio p 158, 254. ch_ch p 45. CLFortin p 270. Colnihko p 263. DeeMPhotography p 114. Dmitry Lityagin p 1, 13, 63, 111, 157, 207, 253. Dashtik p 94. Ekaterina Kondratova p 32, 35, 116, 195, 213. EpicStockMedia p 108. Ekaterina Bratova p 73. Elena Veselova p 21, 41, 70, 125, 135, 169, 247. Elena Shashkina p 4, 12, 88, 295. Edith Frincu p 133. Fired p 181. fullempty p 19. from my point of view p 172. Goskova Tatiana p 232, 251. Gaus Nataliya p 203. homelesscuisine p 53. IrinaMeliukh p 245. istetiana p 83. iuliia_n p 276. Joshua Rainey Photography p 186. Jiri Hera p 190. Julia Sudnitskaya p 220. julie deshaies p 88. Jack Jelly p 201. JeniFoto p 89, 113. Joanna Dorota p 259. HandmadePictures p 166. Kiian Oksana p 61, 165. Karl Allgaeuer p 297. Konstantin Kopachinsky p 25. Levranii p 184. Lilly Trott.jpg OK 85. Larissa Dening p 257. Iocrifa p 269. Liliya Kandrashevich p 241, 243. LENA GABRILOVICH p 299. Iodrakon p 280. Iryna Melnyk p 103. Lisovskaya Natalia p 187, 193. Liv friis-larsen p 201. Magdanatka p 179. marcin jucha p 163. Maria Kovaleva p 44. M. Niebuhr p 126. marcin jucha p 117. Magdanatka p 138. Magdalena Paluchowska p 71. MShev p 97. Nataliya Arzamasova p 55, 62, 110, 123, 141, 145, 246, 273, 275, 283. NoirChocolate p 29. NatashaBreen p 23. nelea33 p 246. nito p 16. Natalia Livingston p 233. Nina Buday p 155. Olga Miltsova 26. Olga Pink p 148. OlenaKaminetska p 205. OlgaPishchulina p 153. Olha Afanasieva p 235. Peredniankina p 287. papkin p 218. Phototasty p 105. Robyn Mackenzie p 101. Rawpixel.com p 6. Robert Kneschke p 278. Romrodphoto p 56. stephanie-frey p 166. Slawomir Fajer p 249. Steiner Wolfgang p 200. Sinkevica p 252. Soloviova Liudmyla p 80. SARYMSAKOV ANDREY p 26. saurabhpbhoyar p 186. successo images p 262. SvetianaFoote p 139. Shaiith p 171. Shaiith p 198.stockcreations p 91. Stepanek Photography p 42. sarsmis p 219. Suzana Marinkovic p 116. Shebeko p 131. Teri Virbickis p 10, 47. Timolina p 174. tuthelens p 69. TunedIn by Westend61 p 276. Tatiana Vorona p 107. TravnikovStudio p 264. Teresa Kasprzycka p 292. teleginatania p 98. TinnaPong p 236. Teleginatania p 189. thefoodphotographer p 210. Victor Moussa p 261. VorontsovaAnastasilia p 121. Vlad Ozerov p 99. Wavebreakmedia p 64. White78 p 232. YuliiaHolovchenko p 147. Yulia Davidovich p 98, 217. Yuliya Gontar p 27. YuliiaKas p 230. Zaitsava Olga p 58. Zkruger p 44. ZinaidaSopina p 222. zi3000 p 167, 285.ziashusha p 134. zstock p 66, 70.
Images used under license from Shutterstock.com

hazelnuts
spiced choc 'n' nut slice 154
herbs 239
honey
honey roast vegetables and crispy
potatoes 204
jam 58
real english scones 60
kiwi fruit
green smoothie bowl 36
lamb
lamb and mushroom pasties 284
leek
chedder and leek mini quiches 102
lentils
red lentil soup 216
lime
avocado lime cheesecake 274
mango
fish tacos with mango salsa 178
mango and coconut balls 140
mango coconut slice 122
matcha
hulk balls 142
millet
millet and pumpkin porridge 50
mushrooms
lamb and mushroom pasties 284
mushroom risotto 192
mushroom soup 214
mushroom tartlets 90
savoury muffins 28
nut crumbs 281
nuts, see also almonds, walnuts
dried fruit bars 132
hulk balls 142
spiced choc 'n' nut slice 154
waffles with fresh fruit and nuts 52
oats
glazed oatmeal cookies 120
pumpkin oat bars 96
orange
simple marmalade 59
pasta
bolognese bake 106
chicken lasagne 240
chicken pasta soup 218
minestrone soup 212
ravioli with green peas and pesto 196
spinach lasagne 248

pastry 223
beef empanadas 226
butterfly puffs 292
chedder and leek mini quiches 102
country-style chicken pie 224
lamb and mushroom pasties 284
mini apple tarts 118
sausage rolls 100
spanakopita (spinach pie) 228
peas
ravioli with green peas and pesto 196
pepitas 33
pineapple
green smoothie bowl 36
grilled fruit 167
Halloween witches' hats 298
pomegranate
waffles with fresh fruit and nuts 52
popcorn
caramel popcorn 262
chocolate popcorn 262
pork
pork spring roll 68
pork dumplings 232
sausage rolls 100
potato
fish cakes 242
honey roast vegetables and crispy potatoes 204
shepherd's pie 244
takeaway fish and chips 170
prawns 187
prawn gyoza 234
sweet and sour prawns 186
pumpkin 95
chicken pumpkin kebab 164
millet and pumpkin porridge 50
pumpkin oat bars 96
pumpkin pikelets 98
pumpkin seeds 33
quinoa
black bean, corn and quinoa salad 182
raisins
dried fruit bars 132
glazed oatmeal cookies 120
walnut and raisin cookies 124
raspberries
overnight raspberry chia pots 34
yoghurt berry cereal pops 135

rice 191
carrot risotto 188
mushroom risotto 192
toasted wraps with rice and vegetables 74
rice paper 67
miso chicken rolls 70
pork spring roll 68
soup 211, see also soup ingredients
spinach 27
green smoothie bowl 36
spanakopita (spinach pie) 228
spinach lasagne 248
strawberries
simple strawberry jam 59
sugar substitutes 129
sunflower seeds 33
sweet potato
home-made veggie chips 89
upside down muffins 286
thyme 200
tofu
marinated tofu 70
tomato
bolognese bake 106
chilli con carne with cheese 180
meatballs in tomato sauce 246
minestrone soup 212
sweet chilli sauce 166
tomato sauce 247
vanilla
garden cupcakes 292
home-made ice cream 277
home-made ice-cream sandwiches 260
princess cupcakes 256
walnuts
easy banana nut muffins 46
energy balls 144
walnut and raisin cookies 124
yoghurt
banana yoghurt popsicles 40
yoghurt berry cereal pops 135
zucchini 81
baked zucchini chips 88
flourless chocolate muffins 84
pizza verde on cauliflower crust 168
savoury muffins 28
upside down muffins 286
zucchini bread 88
zucchini fritters 82
zucchini quiche 86

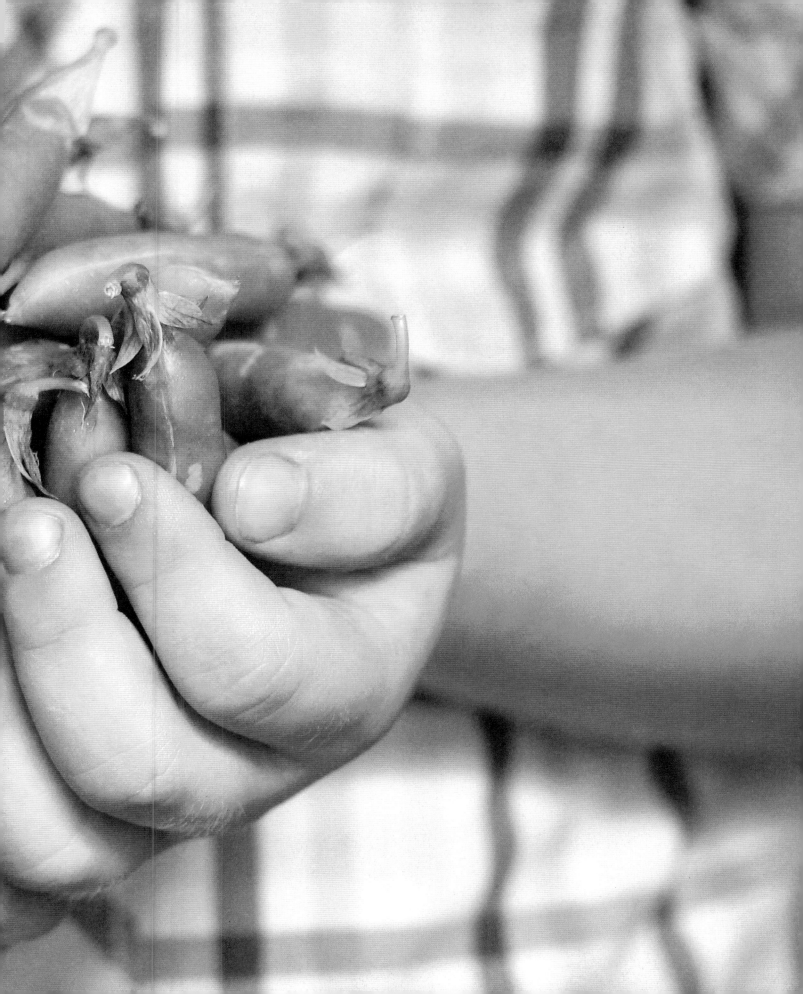

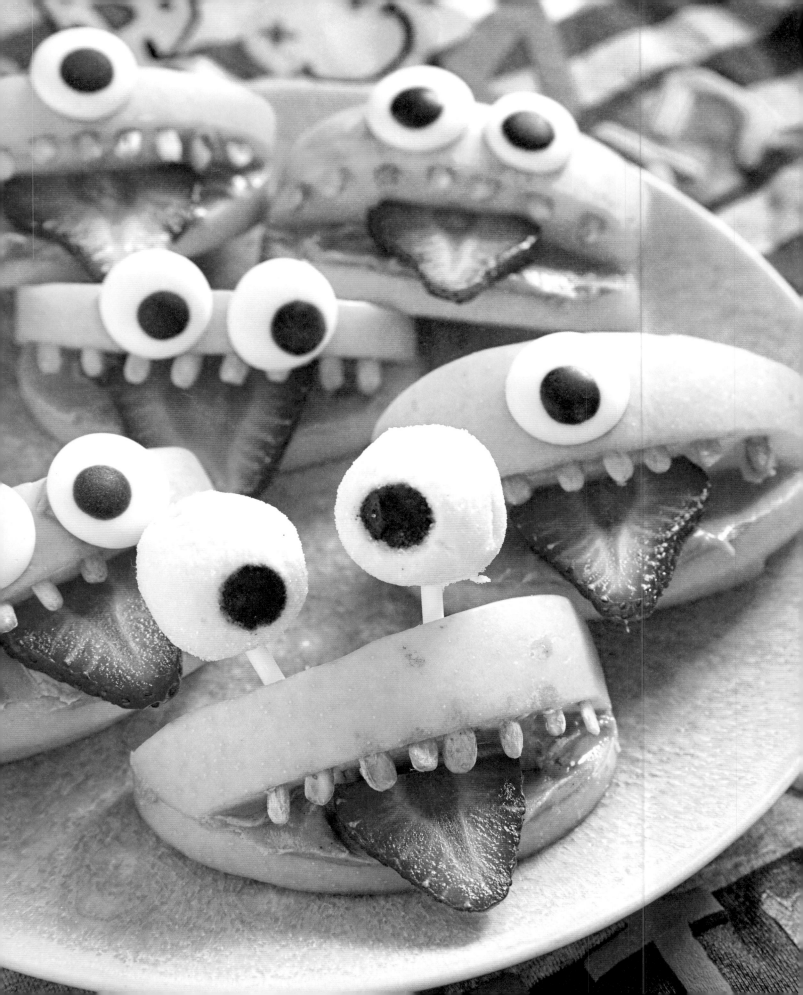

# CONTENTS

Introduction  7

Healthy Breakfasts  13

Lunchboxes  63

Low-Sugar Sweets  111

School-Night Dinners  157

Freezer Friendly  207

Let's Party  253

Index  302

# INTRODUCTION

Cooking for the family can be a challenge at times, even for the most enthusiastic chef. Passion is one thing, but time is another and every mum knows the juggling act that comes with being a carer of kids, hubby and home at the same time as maintaining friendships and employment outside the home. Folding the seamless production of three meals a day for a family into this agenda can sometimes leave us feeling overwhelmed. To make matters worse, it seems these days we are bombarded by information about what we should and shouldn't feed our families for their optimum health and wellbeing. It's no wonder we resort to packaged food and takeaway sometimes.

But that doesn't need to be the case and we hope this book will become a source of support for you in planning how to feed your family. And of course as a busy mum or dad it is all about the planning. As parents we are ever vigilant — and the same is true in the kitchen. Be on the lookout for ways to make your life easier, whether by making breakfast the night before and letting it soak in the fridge overnight, making more than you need at dinner time and freezing the leftovers, or including the kids as you cook or bake, turning it into an activity that might create lasting memories, as well as delicious cupcakes.

This book is divided into six sections that focus on the key food priorities for busy mums and dads. They are breakfast, lunchboxes, low-sugar treats, school-night dinners, freezer-friendly food and party food.

When it comes to breakfast, we provide you with lots of ideas to help you think outside the oatmeal-and-cereal box at breakfast time. There are recipes here that will make for simple, delicious and high-energy breakfasts — try the millet and pumpkin porridge or the raspberry chia pots to ensure that your kids get off to school with plenty of fuel for the day ahead. As you'd expect the focus here is on ease of preparation — you'll find fuss-free recipes for muffins, tortillas and even a breakfast pizza, all of which can be eaten on the go, if necessary. If chia pots sounds unfamiliar, don't worry: we provide a useful overview of key ingredients in this book, especially ones like chia seeds that are becoming increasingly popular but are still a mystery to many.

If you're like every other mum in the world, you'll run out of ideas for the school lunchbox sometimes. For days when inspiration fails to strike, check out the ideas in the lunchbox section of this book. Rice paper rolls might sound complex, but actually they are the opposite: simple to make, very portable, and you can fill them with whatever your kids love to eat (within reason). Rolls in the form of sushi or wraps are another great lunchbox option that we cover in this book. Other favourites such as fritters, muffins, tarts and sausage rolls are covered in this section too. For the hearty eater, how about a slice of bolognaise bake for the lunchbox — a great way to use up leftovers too.

Snacks in the form of muesli bars, biscuits and slices are another hot favourite in the lunchbox, especially with kids, however it can be surprising to read the fine print on the prepackaged varieties: often they contain a lot of sugar as well as a lot of 'numbers'. In this section, you will discover recipes that allow you to easily make low-sugar versions of these treats. The kids won't notice if you sneak a bit of avocado into their chocolate muffin or brownie, and if the

# Family

[fam·i·ly] **adjective**

designed or suitable for both children and adults<family restaurants>

— MERRIAM-WEBSTER

banana loaf tastes good they won't question the type of sugar it contains.

After-school dinners can be a tough assignment — even the most creative mum can run out of ideas by this time of day. Help is at hand in this section with a whole host of family favourite recipes from chilli con carne and lasagna to roast chicken and gravy. The theme section provides ideas for enjoying a family meal, such as a Mexican feast where interesting new flavours can be explored and enjoyed together. And then there's food that can be eaten with the fingers, such as kebabs, grilled fruit and burgers, which is fun for the kids and saves you on the washing up.

While many of the meals in this book are suitable for freezing, the recipe ideas in the 'freezer-friendly' section of the book are particularly geared to this. It's reassuring to have back-up meals and snacks in the freezer for days when life gets too busy for cooking at the end of the day. Soups are a fantastic option for freezing and some soups, like minestrone, are substantial enough for dinner. Tomato sauce, and sauces in general, are a good freezer options too giving you something to throw together with pasta and salad on a weeknight. Pasties, pies and dumplings covered in this section are great to have in the freezer too.

Last but not least, you'll find some great party food options in this book: there are cupcakes, cake pops and popcorn as well as tarts, pasties and nuggets and, for a bit of fun with the kids, recipes for spider eggs, cucumber people and Halloween witches hats.

Enjoy *The Family Life!*

# Healthy Breakfasts

# AMAZING EGGS

Runny eggs, hard-boiled eggs, poached eggs, scrambled eggs, fried eggs … and that's just for breakfast. So versatile, so delicious, the humble egg consists of the yolk, albumen (the white part), shell and chalazae (the blobby strands of egg white that fasten the yolk to the shell membrane). Eggs are like alchemy in baking, providing the basis for custard, fluffy meringue, the aeration in cakes and muffins — and so much more.

## EGGCELLENT NEWS!

As the weight conscious are aware, all the fat is in the yolk (about 5g per egg), while the white contains no fat. Egg white omelettes were a craze that reflected this knowledge. And for some time eggs had a reputation for contributing to heart disease due to cholesterol levels. But not any more. The Heart Foundation's latest review showed that good fats, the polyunsaturated and monounsaturated variety that are found in eggs, are cleansing and remove cholesterol from the bloodstream. An egg a day causes no problems for most people. This means all the family can enjoy eggs regularly as part of a healthy diet! Research confirms the nutritional components of eggs — such as omega-3 fatty acids, protein, folate, and vitamin E.

## STORAGE

Should you store your eggs in the fridge? In the quest for freshness, yes is the general consensus. While you can store eggs safely between 4 and 5°C, storing eggs at room temperature for one day is the same as storing them for a week in the fridge, so only store them at room temperature if you're going to use them that same day. The best way to store eggs is in their original containers in the fridge. The containers will protect against odours from other food items penetrating one of the up to 17,000 tiny pores on the surface of the egg.

A quick test for freshness is to check if the raw egg in the shell sinks in a bowl of water. Fresh eggs stay at the bottom of the bowl while older eggs float because of the large air cell that forms in their base.

## TYPES OF EGGS

It used to be so simple, didn't it? Eggs were eggs until we discovered more about farming methods. And then consumers needed to know a bit more about their eggs and care a little more about the mother hen who laid them. Here is an overview of the most common options available:

CAGE EGGS: These eggs are laid by hens that are permanently housed in a shed inside specially designed cages where their environment is constantly maintained.

BARN-LAID EGGS: The hens that lay these eggs are housed inside large sheds fitted with nests and perches. The hens are free to move around the shed.

FREE-RANGE EGGS: These are laid by hens that roost and lay eggs in a shed, but are also free to wander outside on the farm during the day.

ORGANIC FREE-RANGE EGGS: From accredited organic farms, these eggs are laid by hens that eat an organic diet and are free to roam around outside. Organic is expensive, but there are some foods that might just be worth it. Do eggs fall into this category? They do if you care about the chook. Organic eggs come from chickens that were given 100% organic feed, free of any agricultural chemical residues. The chickens are also treated humanely, with access to outdoor space to roam. It might taste better and it might just make you feel better too.

## MUM-TO-BE

Eggs are an excellent way for pregnant women to meet their increased nutritional requirements during pregnancy. One serve of eggs provides almost 100% of the additional protein requirements and around a third of the extra kilojoules required during pregnancy and lactation. Eggs are an unbeatable source of folate for mums-to-be.

## LEFTOVER YOLKS AND WHITE

Many recipes call for use of either the yolk or the white, often resulting in the waste of the other part. But there are plenty of great ways to avoid this.

With egg yolks consider making hollandaise sauce or alfredo sauce, use to brush a pie crust, make aioli or power up a smoothie. Outside the kitchen, protein and fat-rich egg yolks make a super hair product — beat half a cup until creamy and use as you would a conditioner, or use as a face mask — all that vitamin A helps repair skin. Failing all that, you can freeze leftover egg yolks but add a good pinch of salt before you do as this will prevent them gelling.

Egg whites are equally versatile — the adventurous cook can use them to make macarons or more everyday dishes such as candied nuts, frittata, pavlova, cupcakes, teacakes or mousse. Egg whites freeze particularly well — a nifty trick is to place them in ice cube trays first of all then transfer to freezer bags or an airtight container when solid. They will keep for several months.

# Baked Egg and Ham Cups

## TRY THESE LITTLE GEMS FOR A FUN AND FILLING BREAKFAST THAT'S JUST TOO EASY!

**MAKES 12**

12 slices of ham, thinly sliced

12 eggs

2 Roma tomatoes, sliced and cut into halves

Pinch of salt

Pinch of fresh black pepper

Micro greens, to garnish

Preheat the oven to 190°C (375°F, Gas Mark 5).

Using a 12-hole muffin tin, line individual muffin holes with the ham slices. Gently crack an egg into each hole, taking care not to break the yolk. Place two halved tomato slices to the side of the eggs.

Season with salt and pepper.

Transfer to the oven to bake for 20 minutes.

Remove from the oven and allow to cool for 2-3 minutes before gently removing from the tin.

Garnish with microgreens and serve.

# Gourmet Ham and Egg Bagels

PERFECT SCRAMBLED EGGS ARE THE STAR IN THIS POSH NOSH VERSION
OF A BREKKIE BAGEL THAT'S GREAT FOR ON-THE-GO

**SERVES 4**

6 eggs, at room temperature

¼ cup (60ml, 2fl oz) cream

Freshly ground salt and black pepper, to season

1 tbsp butter, at room temperature

Small handful watercress (or rocket)

8 thin slices prosciutto

4 wholegrain seeded bagels, split, to serve

Place the eggs and cream in a bowl and season with salt and pepper. Gently whisk by hand using a fork until just beaten. Don't overdo it or else you eggs won't have that nice, creamy texture.

Melt the butter in a frying pan over medium heat. Pour eggs into the pan. Don't start stirring the eggs until you first see them begin to set, then stir gently with a wooden spoon for 2 minutes or until the eggs are just set. During cooking, use a wooden spoon to gently push cooked egg to the centre, tilting the pan around to allow uncooked egg to touch the pan bottom.

Place some watercress or rocket on the flat side of each bagel. Top with two slices of prosciutto and a quarter of the scrambled eggs. Season with salt and pepper to taste and place the other halves of the bagels on top.

Serve immediately or wrap up in brown paper and string for the kids to take on the school bus.

# Stop and Go Tortillas

A FUN START TO THE DAY, THE KIDS WILL LOVE THESE FRESH TORTILLAS — EAT THEM FLAT OR WRAP THEM UP

**SERVES 4**

1¾ cups (215g, 7oz) plain flour

1 tsp salt

¼ cup (60ml, 2fl oz) vegetable oil

½ cup (125ml, 4fl oz) hot water

¼ cup (30g, 1oz) extra flour, to use when rolling out tortilla dough

Avocado, peeled and mashed

¾ cup (175g, 6oz) tomato salsa

8 eggs, fried

Place the flour and salt in a large bowl. Add the oil and hot water. Mix well then turn out onto a clean and lightly floured work surface. Knead for 3 minutes until dough is soft and sticky. Using your hands, form eight small balls from the dough. Sprinkle a little flour on each and then roll out the eight tortillas one by one.

Heat a frying pan over a low-medium heat and dry-cook the tortillas one at a time. If they start to puff up, press them down to expel the air. They only need 30 seconds or so on each side, and are cooked when each side has a few browned marks on it.

Cover each freshly cooked tortilla with a paper towel and stack them on top of each other while you cook the rest.

Spread avocado on four of the tortillas and tomato salsa on tthe other four. Top with a fried egg and serve flat or rolled up.

# Mini Breakfast Pizzas

**SERVES 4**

800g (1¾ lb) pizza dough, in 4 separate balls

2 bunches spinach, washed and chopped

2 tbsps fresh basil, finely chopped

½ cup (120g, 4oz) thick tomato puree

100g (3½ oz) Parmesan cheese, grated

125g (4oz) mozzarella, grated

8 eggs

To make the base, see the pizza dough recipe on page 104 of this book, or simply buy a pre-made dough mix.

Prepare spinach by pouring boiling water over it in a colander over the sink. When cool enough to handle squeeze to remove extra liquid. Add basil and mix.

Preheat the oven to 220°C (425°F, Gas Mark 7). Flatten each dough ball to form bases. Push out the edges to form a crust. Spread with tomato puree, then divide spinach mix between the four pizzas. Top with grated Parmesan and mozzarella. Bake each pizza for 5 minutes, then quickly remove from oven and crack two eggs next to each other in the centre. Return the pizzas to the oven to finish cooking until eggs are cooked how you like them.

# The Perfect Boiled Egg

**SERVES 4**

4 eggs, from the fridge

Half fill a saucepan with water and set it over a high heat. Bring the water to a rolling boil.

Lower the heat and reduce to a rapid simmer.

Using a spoon, gently lower the eggs into the water one at a time.

Cook the eggs for 7 minutes.

Remove the eggs with a slotted spoon. Run under a cold tap for 30 seconds.

Place each egg in an egg cup. Use the edge of a knife to gently tap around the top and then slice to remove.

Eat the egg straight from the shell with a small spoon or use toast for dipping.

# SPINACH

Want to make sure the family is getting as much nutrition as possible in their meals? Spinach is well known for its nutritional qualities and has always been regarded as a plant with remarkable abilities to restore energy, increase vitality and improve the quality of the blood. There are sound reasons why spinach would produce such results, primarily the fact that it is rich in iron. But, be warned, frozen spinach may have around half the iron content of fresh.

# Savoury Muffins

FILLING, QUICK AND EASY VEGETARIAN TREATS THAT
MAKE A GREAT BREAKFAST - ON - THE - GO

**MAKES 12**

1 cup (125g, 4oz)
plain flour

1 cup (125g, 4oz)
wholemeal plain flour

1 tbsp baking powder

¼ tsp salt

²⁄₃ cup (80g, 3oz)
Parmesan cheese,
grated

²⁄₃ cup (80g, 3oz)
Cheddar cheese, grated

2 tbsps basil leaves,
finely chopped

6-8 semi-sundried
tomatoes, chopped

2 small zucchinis,
coarsely grated

1 cup (75g, 3oz)
mushrooms, chopped

Freshly ground black
pepper, to taste

¾ cup (185ml, 6fl oz)
milk

⅓ cup (80ml, 3fl oz)
light olive oil

2 eggs

Preheat the oven to 190°C (375°F, Gas Mark 5). Grease a 12-hole muffin tin with oil or butter.

Sift together the flours, baking powder and salt into a large bowl. Gently mix through the Parmesan, cheese, basil, semi-sundried tomatoes, zucchini and mushrooms. Season well with pepper and make a well in the centre.

In a separate bowl, use a fork to whisk together the milk, olive oil and eggs. Pour this into the flour mixture and use a flat spatula or large metal spoon to mix together until just combined. You want the mixture to have lumps in it. Too much mixing makes the muffins tough.

Spoon the mixture evenly into the prepared muffin holes.

Bake in oven for 30 minutes or until the muffins are lightly browned on top and a skewer inserted in the centre comes out clean. Leave to cool in the tin for 5 minutes before transferring to a wire rack. Serve warm or at room temperature.

**NOTE:** These muffins are best eaten the day they are baked, but you can freeze them for up to 3 months. Wrap individually in plastic wrap and seal in an airtight container.

# SUPER SEEDS

Sprinkle some of these super seeds onto their cereal and the kids will be out the door and off to school in no time.

## CHIA SEEDS

These tiny black or white seeds, packed full of protein, healthy fat, fibre, minerals, vitamins and antioxidants, are famous for their energy-boosting properties. If you are not familiar with them yet, here are a few simple ideas for using them:

- Soak in water so they form a gel and store in a sealed container in the fridge (good for 3-4 days), then eat as is for a snack or add to cereal.
- Add a spoonful to whatever smoothie you are making — the kids will never notice!
- Put them in muffins or cakes.
- Due to their gelatinous texture when soaked, chia seeds are great in puddings.

Can't think what to do with them at the moment? Don't worry, put them back in the cupboard: they last for up to 2 years without even being refrigerated, thanks to high antioxidant levels.

## FLAXSEED

Flaxseed, otherwise known as linseed, come from flax, one of the oldest crops in the world. They're high in healthy fat, antioxidants and fibre, and, okay, this might not sound nice but 'mucilage gum content' … and that's good why? Because mucilage in the stomach stops it from emptying too quickly, giving ample time for nutrients to be absorbed.

## SUNFLOWER SEEDS

Crunchy, nutty, yummy and byproduct of the glorious sunflower, what's not to love about this little nutritional powerhouse? Like the other super seeds you'll find here, these little gems are loaded with antioxidants. Sprinkle them on muesli or yoghurts, pop into salads or sneak into muffins and pizza dough. Try toasting them for extra flavour. Sunflower seeds make an excellent, inexpensive alternative to pine nuts.

## PEPITAS

Just to clear up any confusion, pepitas are pumpkin seeds that have been shelled. Sure, you can buy the unshelled version but what kind of mum has time for hulling? You can buy these nutty little green seeds at the supermarket or health-food shop, and enjoy the health benefits of a good source of beta carotene, omega-3, protein, minerals, magnesium, manganese, iron, zinc, copper and vitamin K.

# Overnight Raspberry Chia Pots

WITH BREAKFAST DONE THE NIGHT BEFORE, THESE YUMMY LITTLE FRUIT POTS HAVE 'LIE-IN' WRITTEN ALL OVER THEM

**SERVES 2**

2 cups (250g, 8oz) fresh raspberries

1 orange, peeled and pith removed, roughly chopped

1½ cups (375ml, 13fl oz) almond milk

¼ cup (40g, 1½ oz) white chia seeds

1 tsp vanilla extract

1 cup (90g, 3oz) crunchy granola

2 tbsps maple syrup (optional)

Using a high-speed blender or a food processor, process the raspberries (reserving a generous handful to serve), orange and half of the almond milk until smooth.

Divide the mixture between two serving jars or glasses, then pour half the remaining almond milk, chia seeds and vanilla extract into each jar.

Cover and transfer to the fridge for 1 hour. Stir and then return to the fridge overnight.

To serve, spoon granola and pile raspberries on top of each pot, and drizzle with maple syrup, if using.

# Green Smoothie Bowl

GET THE DAY OFF TO A GREAT START WITH THIS VERSATILE SMOOTHIE BOWL — KIDS, CHOOSE YOUR OWN TOPPINGS!

**SERVES 2**

## SMOOTHIE

2 cups (400g, 14oz) fresh pineapple, chopped

2 bananas, peeled

1 small bunch spinach, washed

2 kiwi fruit, peeled

½ ripe avocado, peeled and pitted

1 tbsp spirulina (optional)

## TOPPINGS

Handful of blueberrues

1 kiwi fruit, peeled and chopped

1 green apple, cored and thinly sliced

2 tbsps desiccated coconut

2 tsps chia seeds

1 tbsp rolled oats

Sprig of fresh mint

Place ingredients for the smoothie into a blender and process until smooth.

Pour the smoothie into 2 bowls and finish with the suggested toppings, or toppings of your choice.

**NOTE:** Using frozen rather than fresh banana will give the smoothie a thicker consistency.

# Activated Almond Milk

ACTIVATE YOUR FAMILY WITH THIS WHOLESOME, CREAMY ALMOND MILK,
PERFECT FOR DAIRY-FREE DIETS

**SERVES 2**

**TO ACTIVATE**

1 cup (125g, 4oz) almonds

Water, for soaking

**NUT MILK**

2 cups (500ml, 1pt) water

½ tsp salt

Honey or maple syrup, to taste (optional)

Place the nuts in a bowl or glass jar and cover with enough water to sit about 2cm (1in) above the nuts. Place a plate or clean tea towel over the top and set aside to soak at room temperature for 12-24 hours. Soaking will activate the almonds.

Drain nuts and rinse well under cool water. Discard the soaking liquid.

Place the almonds, water and salt in a blender. Pulse a few times to break up the almonds, then process at the highest possible speed for 1-2 minutes, until smooth and creamy.

Line a strainer with an opened nut bag or cheese cloth, and place over a measuring cup or bowl. Pour the almond mixture into the strainer and press with the back of a spoon to extract all the milk. If using a nutbag, squeeze to extract as much almond milk as possible.

Add sweetener to taste, if using.

**NOTES:** Soaking for longer will result in creamier milk.

Refrigerate almond milk and be aware that it does not last like cow's milk does. Store in sealed containers in the fridge for 2-3 days.

# Banana Yoghurt Popsicles

GET THE KIDS OUT OF BED AND OFF TO SOCCER PRACTICE QUICK - SMART WITH THESE FROZEN BREAKFAST TREATS

**MAKES 12**

500g (1lb 2oz) Greek yoghurt

1 tbsp maple syrup

3 ripe bananas

2½ (390g, 13 oz) cups dark cooking chocolate

12 icy-pole sticks

Place the yoghurt into a medium-sized bowl and stir in the maple syrup.

Mash the banana until it's as smooth as you can make it and mix into the yoghurt.

Pour the yoghurt mixture evenly into icy-pole moulds. Place an icy-pole stick into the middle of each.

Place the icy poles into the freezer for at least 3 hours, or overnight.

When the icy poles are frozen, melt the chocolate. Break up the chocolate into small pieces and place in a tall, narrow, microwave-safe bowl. Microwave for 30 seconds. Stir well with a rubber spatula, then microwave again for 15 seconds. Stir well, and repeat until the chocolate is smooth. Allow to cool briefly.

Remove the icy poles from the moulds by running briefly under hot water and then pulling the sticks firmly. Don't wiggle the sticks too much or they may break.

Working one at a time, dip the icy poles in the melted chocolate and set on a baking tray lined with baking paper.

Once all of the icy poles have been dipped, place the tray in the freezer for about 10 minutes until the chocolate is set.

# Buckwheat Pancakes

**SERVES 4**

1 cup (125g, 4oz) buckwheat flour

½ tsp sea salt

2 cups (500ml, 1pt) water

¼ tsp vanilla extract

Olive oil or coconut oil, for frying

Place flour and salt into a medium-sized mixing bowl. Gradually add water and vanilla and stir using a whisk until batter is smooth with no lumps. Use immediately or leave the mixture to settle for 20 minutes or so if you have chores to do!

Heat a pan over medium-high heat and add about a teaspoon of oil. Pour batter onto the hot pan, swirling the pan until the surface is just covered.

Cook for 2 minutes or until the surface starts to show small bubbles. Flip and cook the other side for around a minute until golden brown.

# Sticky Sweet Bananas

**SERVES 2**

1 tbsp butter

3 tbsps light brown sugar

2 medium-small firm bananas, halved lengthwise

¼ cup (60ml, 2fl oz) orange juice

Pinch of ground cinnamon

Toast, to serve

Melt butter in a large frying pan over a medium-high heat. Sprinkle in the brown sugar and then place the banana slices on top, cut side up.

Cook undisturbed for 30 seconds, then add orange juice and cinnamon. Cook for 30 seconds, then turn bananas carefully using tongs and cook for a further 1 minute, basting with the pan sauce.

Serve on toast and drizzle over some of the pan sauce.

# BANANAS

A great choice for breakfast, bananas contain energy-boosting carbohydrate and good-for-you protein, vitamins, folate, potassium and magnesium. And if you are expecting an addition to your family, don't forget to have a banana! It's the perfect snack for mums-to-be, providing the extra boost of energy you need to get through the day.

# Easy Banana Nut Muffins

THE KIDS WILL GOBBLE UP THESE MOIST AND MOREISH MUFFINS —
SO FAST THEY WON'T EVEN NOTICE THE HEALTHY CHIA SEEDS!

**MAKES 10**

2 tbsps chia seeds

6 tbsps water

2 bananas, mashed

1 tbsp honey

½ tsp vanilla extract

¼ cup (60ml, 2fl oz) coconut oil (melted)

¼ cup (60ml, 2fl oz) almond milk

1 cup (125g, 4oz) walnuts, roughly chopped

⅓ cup (40g, 1½ oz) coconut flour

½ tsp baking soda

⅛ tsp baking powder

Place the chia seeds in a small bowl. Cover with the water and set aside to soak in for 20 minutes until a gel forms.

Preheat oven to 180°C (350°F, Gas Mark 4). Prepare a 10 holes of a muffin tray by greasing or lining with muffin cases.

Place the chia gel, bananas, honey, vanilla extract, coconut oil and almond milk in a mixing bowl and stir to combine.

Place the walnuts, flour, baking soda and baking powder together in a large mixing bowl.

Add the wet ingredients to the bowl containing the dry ingredients. Stir to combine, ensuring all ingredients are incorporated.

Scrape the batter into the prepared muffin tray, and transfer to the oven to bake for 15 minutes, until a skewer inserted in the centre comes out clean and the top looks toasty.

# GLUTEN-FREE FLOURS

You've noticed that gluten is not exactly popular these days. 'What does that mean for my breakfast pancakes?' Fear not help is on hand with these gluten-free alternatives.

## BUCKWHEAT FLOUR

First up, what is this flour made from? The answer is buckwheat groats that have been milled and sieved to remove the tough husk. Compared to regular plain flour, it's darker in colour, nuttier in taste and denser in texture, so while it tastes wonderful the resulting pancake may be heavier than you are used to. Experiment with quantities and also mixing with other products such as almond meal for a fluffier result. Buckwheat flour is a big high five on the nutrient and anti-inflammatory front, although it is a little more expensive than regular plain flour.

## RICE FLOUR

No prizes for guessing what rice flour is made of: rice of course — that's been finely ground. It's bright white in colour, and fine and powdery in texture. Commonly used in Indian recipes that call for a light batter, rice flour can also be used as a thickener in sauces, a base for baked goods and as a substitute for plain flour when breading fish or schnitzel.

## ALMOND FLOUR

Almond flour has its detractors, particularly those that point out its high caloric value: a cup contains about 90 almonds, with an estimated value of over 600 calories. Woah. Not for the weight conscious. On the up side, it's high in protein and super tasty. Note that due to the high oil content of this flour, it's best to use it quickly or store in the fridge, allowing it to come to room temperature before using.

## AMARANTH FLOUR

Produced by grinding seeds from the amaranth plant, this fine flour is nutty and earthy in flavour. Interesting fact: amaranth flour has twice as much calcium as cow's milk so it's a good choice for the lactose intolerant looking to increase calcium levels.

## CHICKPEA FLOUR

Also called besan or gram flour, this gluten-free alternative is high in protein, iron and fibre. Unique among the gluten-free flours, chickpea flour is naturally dense which gives it inherent binding power, so it's a good choice for baked goods such as breads, cakes and muffins.

# Millet and Pumpkin Porridge

A GLUTEN-FREE, FLAVOURFUL AND PROTEIN-PACKED PORRIDGE TO KICKSTART YOUR FAMILY'S DAY

**SERVES 4**

1 tbsp vegetable oil

1 cup (190g, 7oz) dry hulled millet

2¼ cups (560ml, 1pt 2fl oz) boiling water

½ tsp salt

¼ cup (30g, 1oz) slivered almonds

1 cup (250ml, 8fl oz) milk

1 cup (225g, 8oz) cooked and pureed butternut pumpkin

1-2 tbsps maple syrup

1 tsp vanilla essence

½ tsp cinnamon

¼ tsp nutmeg

Heat oil in a medium saucepan over medium-high heat. Add the millet and stir for 2 minutes to coat it in oil. Add the boiling water and the salt, reduce to a simmer and cook for 20 minutes, stirring frequently, until the water is absorbed and the millet is tender. Add more water if needed.

While the millet simmers, toast the almonds in a frying pan until lightly browned, for about 3 minutes.

Stir the milk into the warm millet. Then add the pumpkin, maple syrup, vanilla, cinnamon, nutmeg and almonds. Gently heat and mix through until the millet has absorbed most of the milk and the mix is creamy.

Portion porridge into four bowls and serve with maple syrup and milk on the side.

# Waffles with Fresh Fruit and Nuts

CLASSIC BELGIAN WAFFLES WITH FRESH TOPPINGS MAKE THIS A GREAT CHOICE FOR A HEALTHY SUNDAY BRUNCH FOR YOUR FAMILY

**SERVES 4**

2 cups (250g, 8oz) plain flour

¾ cup (165g, 6oz) caster sugar

3 tsps baking powder

½ tsp salt

2 large eggs, separated

2 cups (500ml, 1pt) buttermilk

½ cup (125ml, 4fl oz) canola or vegetable oil

1 tsp vanilla extract

**TO SERVE**

Sliced banana

Pomegranate seeds

Cashews and almonds

In a bowl, combine flour, sugar, baking powder and salt and make a well.

In another bowl, lightly beat the egg yolks. Add buttermilk, oil and vanilla and mix well.

Stir the milk mixture into the dry ingredients with a spatula or large spoon until combined.

Beat egg whites until stiff peaks form and fold gently into the batter. Try your best to keep the mix light and fluffy.

Cook in a preheated waffle iron for at least 2 minutes or until golden brown. Before transferring to a plate, hold the waffle in your tongs for about 10 seconds to release excess steam — this helps keep them crispy.

Serve waffles with sliced banana, pomegranate and nuts.

# Cauliflower Hash Browns

SNEAK SOME GOODNESS INTO THE KIDS WITH THIS
HEALTHY TAKE ON A PERENNIAL BRUNCH FAVE

**SERVES 4**

1 head cauliflower

2 eggs

2 tbsps dill

½ cup (60g, 2oz) Parmesan cheese, grated

½ tsp salt

2 tbsps butter

Preheat oven to 220°C (430°F, Gas Mark 7).

Roughly chop the cauliflower and process in a food processor or blender on until it reaches a fine, rice-like consistency.

Transfer to a bowl and microwave for 2 minutes. Set aside to cool a few minutes.

Place a clean tea towel onto your bench and transfer the cauliflower rice into the centre. Twist the towel into a tight knot and press out as much water as you can.

In a bowl, whisk the eggs. Mix in the cauliflower, dill, cheese and salt.

Heat butter in a frying pan on medium heat until melted. Drop 1 tablespoon of the batter into the pan. Press down gently to form a patty.

Fry for 2 minutes on each side, then remove from the frying pan and place on paper towels to drain.

Toast in the oven for 2-3 minutes on each side for an extra crispy finish.

# THE SETTING POINT

Grandmas the world over will give you top tips on jam-making, but most will agree a critical factor is knowing the setting point of your jam. With experience you can recognise when a fast, frothy boil starts to calm to a more relaxed boil. The surface will be glossier, with no air bubbles and the mixture will seem thicker. Test by chilling saucers in the freezer and dropping jam onto them. Wait for half a minute then hold the saucer vertically. Does the jam slowly slide down? That's okay for a light set jam, or return it to the pan to thicken further. Does the jam hold firm on the saucer and wrinkle when pressed? That's a firmer set jam. Too firm and the jam will lose its delicate flavour. Not firm enough, well, you could call it syrup and serve on pancakes!

# Simple Strawberry Jam

MAKES 2 JARS

2 x 250g (9oz) punnets of strawberries

3 tbsps lemon juice

1½ cups (330g, 12oz) sugar

This jam can be made in the microwave. First prepare the fruit by washing and hulling the strawberries. Then pop the strawberries and lemon juice in a large microwave-friendly bowl. Cook on high for 3 minutes to soften the fruit, then add the sugar and stir the mixture before returning to the microwave to cook on high for a further 20 minutes. Check the mixture occasionally to ensure it isn't overflowing.

At the 20-minute mark, test the jam by dropping a little on a cold saucer. It should form a gel. If it's still too wet, return to the microwave for another 5 minutes and then check again. Repeat until a firm gel forms when dropped on the plate.

Remove from the microwave and stir to ensure sugar is mixed through. Allow to cool slightly then carefully transfer into sterilised jars and seal.

NOTE: Jam will keep for up to 4 weeks in the fridge.

# Simple Marmalade

MAKES 3 JARS

1kg (2lb) oranges

3 cups (750ml, 24fl oz) water

1kg (2lb) sugar

Clean the oranges by running under cold water and scrubbing with a clean cloth. Peel two of the oranges and finely chop the peel. Set peel aside. Peel the remaining oranges and transfer the flesh of all the oranges to a food processor or high-speed blender. Process until oranges have formed a pulp with some lumps remaining.

Place a saucepan over a high heat and add orange pulp and peel to the pan. Pour over the water and bring to the boil. Reduce heat slightly, then cover the pan, and allow to cook on a rapid simmer for 20 minutes.

Place a saucer in the freezer now to use for testing.

Gradually pour the sugar into the pan, stirring constantly. Increase heat again and boil vigorously for 15 minutes.

Spoon a drop of marmalade onto the chilled plate to test for readiness. It should gel on contact with the plate. If not, return to the boil for 5 minutes then test again until ready. Set aside to cool slightly before transferring to sterilised jars.

# Real English Scones

BREAKFAST LIKE ROYALTY WITH THESE DELICIOUS HOME-MADE ENGLISH SCONES — PERFECT WITH BUTTER AND STRAWBERRY JAM

**SERVES 4**

2 cups (250g, 8oz) flour

4 tsps baking powder

½ tsp salt

3 tbsps caster sugar

90g (3oz) unsalted butter, cubed, at room temperature

⅔ cup (160ml, 5fl oz) milk

1 large egg

3 tbsps granulated sugar

Strawberry or other desired jam, to serve

Preheat the oven to 220°C (425°F, Gas Mark 7).

In a food processor, pulse the flour, baking powder, salt and sugar a couple times to combine.

Add the butter and pulse until the butter is completely mixed through. The mixture should look like fine breadcrumbs. Transfer to a large mixing bowl.

In a small bowl, whisk the milk and egg together. Reserve 2 tablespoons for the scone glaze and pour the rest in with the flour mixture.

Stir to combine with a wooden spoon until it comes together to form a dough. Transfer to a lightly floured benchtop and knead until the dough becomes smooth then form into a smooth ball. Keep flouring the bench as needed to keep the surface of the dough from getting sticky.

Roll the dough out about 2cm (1in) thick (this is important!) and use a 5cm (2in) diameter round cutter to cut rounds out of the dough. Keep re-rolling the dough out and cutting into rounds until the dough is used up.

Place the scones onto a lined baking tray and brush the tops with the reserved milk and egg mix. Sprinkle with sugar.

Bake the scones for 12 minutes, until about tripled in height, and golden brown on the tops and bottoms.

Serve with lashings of butter and jam!

# Lunchboxes

# RICE PAPER ROLLS

The rice paper for making your rolls is readily available from supermarkets these days. That's lucky because, let's face it, you're too busy to soak, grind and pound rice into a pliable paste.

These circular, translucent disks are sold dried, but just a quick dip in warm water and they become soft and pliable — amazing! This quality is thanks to the tapioca powder that the rice paper contains, along with rice flour, salt and water.

On its own the rice paper is not particularly nutritious (not bad, but not good either) but what a great opportunity this presents to pack healthy, delicious fillings inside.

A good idea for the fussy kid is to add slices of barbecued chicken inside; just pick up a cooked chook from the supermarket. Few kids can resist this. Eating rice paper rolls is fun and often kids love to dip them in a yummy peanut, fish or sweet chilli sauce, so don't forget to whip up a quick sauce or buy a pre-made version if you are short on time. The typical Vietnamese dipping sauce is a mix of fish sauce, vinegar, sugar, lemon juice and chilli. Hoisin sauce is great in rice paper rolls and the bottled versions are widely available, making this an easy option. A bottle of hoisin sauce comes in handy to make an easy peanut dipping sauce too — just add peanut butter, soy sauce, garlic and water.

## ON A ROLL

Here are some tips to get you rolling smoothly.

- Don't overfill! You should be able to roll without the wrapper falling apart, so if this happens start again using only fewer ingredients.
- Don't oversoak! You only need to dip the wrapper in warm water for 5 seconds or less. If it becomes too wet, it loses its ability to stick.
- Try to prepare the rolls close to eating, if possible. Otherwise, keep them covered in a cool place but not refrigerated as they will dry out.
- When planning fillings, keep in mind a balance of ingredients and flavours. You want to have a protein, a carbohydrate (like vermicelli noodles) and a vegetable. Ideally, you'll have crunch, sweetness and saltiness in one roll.

Here are some great ideas for flavour combinations for the kids:

- Prawns and mango
- Avocado and barbecued chicken
- Ham and capsicum
- Tuna and avocado

Or let the kids decide!

# Pork Spring Roll

## SO TASTY AND EASY TO ASSEMBLE — THE KIDS WILL LOVE HELPING YOU PUT THESE TOGETHER

**MAKES 12**

150g (5oz) rice vermicelli

4 eggs, lightly beaten

1 tsp sesame oil

1 clove garlic, chopped

1 tsp fresh ginger, grated

350g (12oz) minced pork (or chicken or beef)

2 tbsps soy sauce

2 tbsps oyster sauce

12 rice paper sheets

Small handful tightly packed fresh coriander leaves, coarsely chopped

Small handful tightly packed mint, coarsely chopped

4 spring onions, thinly sliced

350g (12oz) butter lettuce, finely shredded

¼ cup (60ml, 2fl oz) sweet chilli sauce

2 tbsps lime juice

Bring a medium saucepan of water to the boil, add the vermicelli and cook for 2 minutes until just tender. Drain and leave to cool.

**MAKING THE FILLING**
Using a large non-stick frying pan, make a thin omelette with the eggs. Cook until just set. Remove from pan and set aside to cool.

In the same pan, add the sesame oil and then cook the garlic, ginger and pork. Keep stirring until the meat is cooked through.

Add the soy sauce and oyster sauce and mix through.

While this is cooling, slice the omelette into thin strips, around 10cm (4in) long.

**WRAPPING**
Dip a sheet of rice paper into a large bowl of hot water very quickly to soften it. Let it sit for about 30 seconds to dry. You can have about four sheets on the go at a time and they shouldn't dry out too much.

Place a dessertspoon of the meat filling mixture in a long strip along the middle of the rice paper. Place a similar amount of vermicelli and one or two egg strips on top as well as a small amount of the coriander, mint, spring onion and lettuce. Be sparing with these as the sheet needs to roll up neatly, although you'll get the hang of how much you need after your first two rolls. Fold each short side of the sheet over the filling. Then from one end roll up the sheet to form the rolls and sit each one on the fold. Repeat with remaining sheets.

**SERVING**
Serve the rolls with dipping sauce made by mixing the sweet chilli sauce, lime juice and any remaining coriander and mint.

# Miso Chicken Rolls

**SERVES 4**

⅓ cup (80ml, 3fl oz) miso paste

2 tsps sesame oil

⅓ cup (80ml, 3fl oz) mirin

3 chicken breasts, trimmed

8 sheets rice paper

2 carrots, julienned

¼ head iceberg lettuce, roughly chopped

1 small cucumber, halved and cut into strips

1 avocado, peeled and sliced

½ red capsicum, cut into strips

Combine miso, oil and mirin in a bowl and mix. Toss chicken through marinade until well coated. On a medium heat, grill chicken for 7-8 minutes on each side until cooked through. Remove and cut into strips.

Fill a large shallow bowl with lukewarm water. Place one rice paper sheet into the water for a few seconds. Gently lift out and place on a flat work surface. Place a little of each vegetable in the middle but slightly to the right of the sheet leaving about 2cm (1in) space on each end. Fold the top and bottom of the sheet over the vegetables and then starting from the right, roll the sheet up into a tight roll. Repeat this for the rest of the rice paper sheets.

# Marinated Tofu

**SERVES 4**

450g (1lb) firm tofu

6 tbsps soy sauce

2 tsps honey

2 tsps balsamic vinegar

1½ tbsps ginger, grated

1 garlic clove, minced

Preheat oven to 200°C (400°F, Gas Mark 6).

Drain tofu and pat dry with paper towel. Slice into small squares of desired thickness.

Mix together soy sauce, honey, vinegar, ginger and garlic.

Place three-quarters of the marinade into a shallow baking dish and add tofu, turning each steak over to ensure tofu is thoroughly coated in marinade.

Once all steaks are covered, pour on remainder of the marinade.

Bake for 30 minutes, until golden and crispy on the outside.

# ALMOND BUTTER

Almond butter is made by blending almonds into a thick spread or paste. Much like peanut butter it can be used on bread, in satays, smoothies, muffins, snacks and health bars. Almond butter is often considered the healthy alternative to peanut butter as it is packed full of vitamins, minerals, fibre and protein and has way less saturated fat than peanut butter. You can pick up a jar of almond butter at the health-food store or supermarket for a quick option, or try making it yourself so you can add your own flavours and leave out any nasties.

# Crunchy Carrot Sushi

THESE HAPPY LITTLE SUSHI-STYLE ROLLS ARE JUST SO EASY TO MAKE, PROVIDING A HEALTHY RAW FOOD OPTION THAT'S SWEET AND JUICY

**SERVES 2**

4 carrots, peeled and roughly chopped

2 tsps apple cider vinegar

2 nori seaweed sheets

½ avocado, peeled, stoned and cut into strips

½ red capsicum, seeded and sliced into strips

1 yellow capsicum, seeded and sliced into strips

⅓ kohlrabi, peeled and sliced into strips (optional)

1 stem Thai basil, leaves picked

Place the carrots in a food processor and process until a rice-like consistency forms. Add the vinegar and process again until combined.

Lay the nori sheets shiny side down on a clean surface and spread the carrot rice mixture onto each sheet until it reaches the edges, leaving a border at the top and bottom.

Place the vegetables and basil at the bottom of each sheet on top of the rice.

Roll from the bottom, using thumbs to roll and fingers to keep the vegetables intact. Apply even and firm pressure.

Dab water or lemon juice at the top of the nori roll to create a seal.

Cut into slices using a very sharp knife.

**NOTE:** Use a bamboo mat to roll the sushi if you have one.

# Toasted Wraps with Rice and Vegetables

MAKE THE FILLING AHEAD OF TIME SO YOU CAN PUT TOGETHER THIS TASTY SNACK WHENEVER THE NEED ARISES

**SERVES 4**

3 tbsps olive oil

1 garlic clove, crushed

½ head cauliflower, finely chopped

80g (3oz) corn kernels

½ cup (80g, 3oz) peas

½ red capsicum, finely chopped

1 cup (155g, 4oz) brown rice

1¼ cups (310ml, 10fl oz) hot vegetable stock

½ tsp dried oregano

½ tsp cumin powder

2 spring onions, sliced

4 mountain bread wraps

Heat 1 tablespoon of the oil in a large saucepan on medium-high heat.

Fry the garlic for 1 minute. Add the cauliflower, corn, peas and red capsicum. Cook for 3 minutes until the vegetables are slightly softened. Remove from the pan.

Add the 2 tablespoons of oil and the rice to the same pan. Stir for 1 minute until the rice is coated with oil and slightly translucent. Add the stock and gently simmer for 40 minutes or until the rice is cooked.

Add the vegetables, spices and spring onions to the rice and stir through. (This mix can be stored in the fridge in an airtight container to use whenever you need it over the next 2-3 days.)

Place ¾ cup of warm rice mixture onto the centre of a warmed piece of mountain bread. Fold the top and bottom of the bread over the rice mixture; fold the sides of the bread towards the centre. Roll up tightly into a wrap.

Place the wrap in a dry, hot grillpan and toast for 2-3 minutes until nicely charred on both sides. Cut in half. Serve immediately.

# Easy Tandoori Chicken Wraps

THE KIND OF SPICY ALL THE FAMILY CAN ENJOY — TASTY BUT NOT BURNING HOT — THESE WRAPS ARE A GREAT LUNCHBOX IDEA

**SERVES 4**

4 tbsps tandoori paste

⅔ cup (150g, 4oz) Greek yoghurt

400g (14oz) chicken breast fillets, sliced

3 tbsps vegetable oil

4 tbsps mint, finely chopped

4 white soft wraps

2 Lebanese cucumbers, thinly sliced

2 small carrots, julienned

80g (3oz) mixed salad leaves

Place the tandoori paste and 1 tablespoon of yoghurt in a medium-sized bowl and stir to combine. Add the chicken and stir to coat. Cook immediately or cover and place in the fridge for 30 minutes to marinate.

Heat oil in a frying pan over moderate heat until shimmering. Add chicken and cook for 1-2 minutes, turning once to get some colour on the meat. Reduce heat slightly and cook for a further 4 minutes until cooked through.

Place the mint and remaining yoghurt in a small bowl and stir to combine. Spread the mixture on the surface of each wrap. Place chicken in the centre, and then salad ingredients. Tuck one end over using your fingers to keep the ingredients in place and then roll to enclose the filling. Cut wraps in half to serve.

**NOTE:** If the wraps need to be softened you can do this by microwaving them on medium heat for 30 seconds. To soften multiple wraps at once, separate them with paper towel.

# ZUCCHINI

This vibrant, green veggie — a great source of vitamin A for good eyesight, fibre for digestion and magnesium for happy muscles — is versatile as well as valuable. For a children's party, mini zucchini pancakes or muffins are always a winner. Little ones who think they don't love vegetables will barely know — zucchini is so mild in flavour, they might think they're eating apples.

Here are some great ideas for working the humble zucchini into your menu.

ZUCCHINI CAKE: It doesn't taste like vegetables and is especially healthy when baked up with wholewheat or buckwheat flour for extra fibre and protein.

ZUCCHINI SOUP: There are creamy recipes made with cream, which is luxurious and a bit naughty. Then there are smooth soups that are silky even without cream. Let the zucchini soften in butter, garlic, salt and pepper before pureeing to a velvety soup.

ZUCCHINI RIBBONS: these are fun to dangle and twirl, then chomp and eat (for kids as well as adults) and so easy to make. Choose zucchinis that are nice and long. Use a mandolin slicer if it's available or just a nice sharp knife to cut thin, wide ribbons — cut the vegetable lengthways. Saute lightly in olive oil and pepper and add chopped mint to warm. Garnish with lemon and crumbles of feta cheese.

ZUCCHINI FRIES: The best not-bad-for-anyone hot chips ever. Rub zucchini fingers with egg and roll in a crumb mix of polenta, Parmesan, lemon rind, salt and pepper before frying or oven baking.

## ZUCCHINI PASTA

On pasta night, get sneaky: zucchini's true stand-out dish, especially for parents who are watching the waistline, is otherwise known as zoodles. That is, 'pasta' made from zucchinis. No wheat, gluten or drowsy after-effects.

HOW TO MAKE ZOODLES:

- Cut the zucchini into matchsticks. Skin and all.
- Cook for 1 minute in a pan with olive oil on low to medium heat.
- Turn off the heat. Add water to cover the noodles — about 4 tablespoons. Turn on the heat to half steam, half boil, until the zucchini pasta is just soft.
- Now, it's ready for sauce. Choose a lemony, cheesy olive oil mix or a classic tomato sauce, topped with Parmesan.

Once it's a beloved weekly dish, consider investing in a julienne slicer, a mandolin slicer or a spiraliser.

# Zucchini Fritters

KID-FRIENDLY FRITTERS THAT ARE EASY TO MAKE, EASY TO PACK IN LUNCHBOXES AND EASY TO EAT

**SERVES 4**

2 zucchinis, grated

1 tsp salt

2 eggs, beaten

2 spring onions, finely chopped

2 tbsps fresh dill, finely chopped

100g (3½ oz) feta cheese, crumbled

1 clove garlic, minced

¼ tsp pepper

¼ cup (30g, 1oz) plain flour

½ tsp baking powder

Olive oil, for frying

Toss zucchini with salt and place in a strainer for 10 minutes. Squeeze out excess liquid. Set aside.

Combine the eggs with zucchini, spring onions, dill, feta, garlic and pepper in a large mixing bowl.

Stir in flour and baking powder and mix until thoroughly combined.

Heat olive oil in a large frying pan over a medium heat.

Spoon in 2 tablespoonfuls of batter and flatten the mixture in the pan with the back of a spoon.

Fry for 3 minutes then turn over and fry for a further 2 minutes, until golden. Transfer to a plate lined with a paper towel to absorb grease.

Repeat with remaining batter.

# Flourless Chocolate Muffins

ZUCCHINI PLAYS A STARRING ROLE IN THIS MOIST AND DELICIOUS
CHOCOLATE MUFFIN — A HEALTHY CHOICE FOR LUNCHBOXES

**MAKES 6**

1 cup (170g, 6oz)
zucchini, grated

½ cup (180g, 6oz)
smooth peanut butter

1 very ripe banana

1 egg

¼ cup (90g, 3oz) honey

¼ cup (30g, 1oz) cocoa
powder

2 tbsps ground flaxseed
(or chia seeds)

1 tsp vanilla extract

½ tsp baking soda

¾ cup (120g, 4oz)
chocolate chips

Preheat the oven to 190°C (375°F, Gas Mark 5) and lightly grease
a 6-hole muffin tray.

Squeeze the zucchini and drain off the excess water. Repeat
the process until no more moisture can be extracted from the
zucchini. Set aside.

Place the peanut butter, banana, egg, honey, cocoa powder,
flaxseed, vanilla extract and baking soda in a blender or food
processor, and blend until a smooth batter forms. Stir in zucchini
and a third of the chocolate chips.

Pour the batter into the prepared tray about two-thirds of the
way full. Sprinkle remaining chocolate chips on top.

Place in oven and bake for 35 minutes or until the tops are set
and a skewer inserted into the centre comes out clean.

# Zucchini Quiche

THIS PLEASINGLY SIMPLE QUICHE IS PERFECT FOR WEEKEND LUNCHES AND WEEKDAY LUNCHBOXES

**SERVES 2-4**

1 sheet pre-made shortcrust pastry

1 medium brown onion, finely chopped

1 tbsp olive oil

1 cup (125g, 4oz) packed Cheddar cheese, grated

½ cup (60g, 2oz) Swiss cheese, grated

3 medium zucchinis, grated and well drained

½ cup (60g, 2oz) plain flour

1 tsp salt

4 eggs, beaten

½ cup (125ml, 4fl oz) milk

½ tsp freshly ground black pepper

Preheat oven to 220°C (430°F, Gas Mark 7). Line the base and sides of a 23cm (9in) pie dish with the shortcrust pastry. Trim the edge. Line with baking paper and fill with a baking weight such as rice or beans. Place in the oven to bake for 10 minutes, then remove the baking weights and discard the paper. Return to the oven to bake for a further 6-8 minutes, or until pastry is just golden. Set aside.

Reduce oven temperature to 180°C (350°F, Gas Mark 4).

In a small frying pan, saute the onion in oil until softened and golden.

In a large bowl, add the cheeses, zucchini, onion and flour and salt. Mix well so that all ingredients are evenly distributed.

Add the eggs and milk, ensuring again that everything is thoroughly mixed together.

Pour into the pastry case. Bake in the oven for 30 minutes or until the centre is set.

Sprinkle with black pepper and serve warm.

# Zucchini Bread

**SERVES 6**

3 cups (375g, 12oz) plain flour

2 tsps baking powder

¼ tsp bicarbonate of soda

1 tsp cinnamon

1 tsp salt

2 eggs

1½ cups (240g, 9oz) brown sugar, packed

¾ cup (185ml, 6fl oz) olive oil

2 tsps vanilla extract

2-3 zucchinis, grated and squeezed of excess moisture

Heat the oven to 180°C (350°F, Gas Mark 4). Grease two 20 x 10 x 7cm (8 x 4 x 3in) loaf tins.

Combine the flour, baking powder, bicarb and spices in a large mixing bowl. In a separate bowl, whisk together the eggs, sugar, olive oil and vanilla extract.

Stir the zucchini into the flour mixture. Pour the wet mixture over the top. Gently stir and fold until flour is fully combined. Divide the batter between the two loaf tins. Place in the oven and bake for 45 minutes, until golden brown and a skewer inserted in the centre comes out clean.

# Baked Zucchini Chips

**SERVES 4**

4 zucchinis

2 tbsps olive oil

2 tsps salt

1 tsp paprika

1 tsp cumin

½ tsp cayenne pepper (optional)

Preheat oven to 130°C (265°F, Gas Mark 1).

Slice zucchinis very thinly, as close to paper thin as you can manage. Place the slices in a mixing bowl and sprinkle oil, salt and all the spices over the top. Mix to coat the slices thoroughly.  Try adding olive oil 1 tablespoon at a time as you don't want it to get soggy.

Line a large, flat baking tray with baking paper and place each slice on the sheet. Try to keep them from touching each other to give them enough room to go nice and crispy. Bake for at least 1 hour, checking every 20 minutes or so and flipping them over half way.

Once the slices are browned and crispy, take them out and let them cool down on the tray for 2 minutes to allow excess moisture to evaporate.

# HOME - MADE VEGGIE CHIPS

Why stick to corn or potato chips when there are so many colourful and nutritious vegies you can use? Zucchini, sweet potato, kale, parsnip and beetroot are all perfect for slicing thinly and baking into chips and will satisfy any chip craving. Homemade chips are a healthy alternative to packaged snacks and will get wolfed down so quickly you won't ever have to say the phrase 'eat your veggies' again. Plus, they're a fantastic gluten- and dairy-free option for those with sensitive stomachs.

# Mushroom Tartlets

THESE BITE-SIZED AND DELICIOUS LITTLE TARTLETS MAKE AN IDEAL LUNCH OR LUNCHBOX FILLER

**SERVES 6**

### PASTRY

1¼ cups (155g, 5oz) plain flour

¼ tsp salt

8 tbsps cold butter, chopped

4 tbsps very cold water

### FILLING

½ tsp salt

1 tsp olive oil

1 tbsp butter

3 leeks, chopped, white part only

1 capsicum, deseeded and chopped

Pinch of salt

250g (9oz) button or Swiss brown mushrooms, sliced

1 cup (250ml, 8fl oz) thickened cream

2 eggs, beaten

¼ tsp pepper

½ cup (60g, 2oz) Cheddar or Parmesan cheese, grated

Combine flour and salt in a large bowl. Add butter and rub with fingertips until it resembles coarse crumbs. Gradually add water, until the mixture begins to hold together. Gather the dough into a ball and flatten into a thick disk. Wrap in plastic wrap and refrigerate for 30 minutes.

Preheat oven to 220°C (425°F, Gas Mark 7) and grease six springform tartlet pans and one baking tray.

Turn pastry onto a floured surface and roll out thinly. Cut circles from the pastry using a floured round cutter. Press pastry into tartlet tins and trim edges. Prick bottom of pastry shells with a fork. Line the pastry with baking paper, and fill with dried beans, then place in the oven and blind bake for 20 minutes. Remove beans and paper and return to oven to bake for a further 10 minutes. Remove from oven and cool completely on a wire rack.

Melt the butter in a large frying pan over a medium heat. Add leeks, capsicum and a pinch of salt. Cook, stirring, for 3 minutes until the vegetables have softened. Add the mushrooms and cook for a further 2-3 minutes until mushrooms are tender.

Combine cream, eggs, cooked vegetables and pepper in a medium bowl. Pour the mixture into the pastry crusts and sprinkle cheese on top.

Place in the oven and bake for 30 minutes, until pastry is nicely browned, filling is set and cheese is golden on top. Cool on a wire rack.

# PUMPKIN

Pumpkin is a super versatile vegetable — it can be mushy enough for very young mouths or it can be steamed to preserve its texture. It will caramelise with oil and heat. It also absorbs flavours beautifully so makes a brilliant base for dinnertime and dessert dishes — cumin and cinnamon are excellent seasonings.

There are several popular varieties, including butternut pumpkin, Japanese pumpkin and golden nugget pumpkin and all are bursting with vitamin A for eye health, vitamin C for the immune system, fibre for healthy tummies and beta-carotene which acts like a natural moisturiser with a mild sunscreen for youthful skin at all ages. (Of course, don't skip out on the SPF 30+ for long days in the sun.)

## IN THE KITCHEN

MAKE A SMOOTHIE: Stir 1 cup pumpkin puree into plain Greek yoghurt. Add vanilla essence and a dash of maple syrup. Layer with muesli or granola for more oomph.

SUGAR-AND-SPICE SEEDS: Toss seeds in melted butter, sugar, cinnamon, nutmeg and allspice. Bake until golden brown — about 30 minutes.

PANCAKES THE COLOUR OF SUNSET: Add ½ cup pumpkin puree and ¼ teaspoon each of nutmeg and cinnamon to batter. The pancakes are sweet with white flour and nutty with whole wheat flour.

## OUTSIDE FUN TIMES

Carving pumpkins is all the rage at Halloween and the results are always fun. However, the process can be a challenge — cutting into a pumpkin takes strong muscles and sharp knives. Why not use the sturdy, shiny skin as a canvas and decorate the outside.

SILHOUETTES: Buy or create black stencils in the shapes of bats or broomsticks or any intriguing shape for any time of year. Paint the pumpkins white, then glue the stencils around the pumpkin for a silhouette effect.

POLKA DOT PUMPKINS: Use all the dot-like items around the house — buttons, stickers, beads or round lollies like chocolate drops. Take the glue to the pumpkin and let the kids loose with their spotty vision.

PUMPKIN PEOPLE: These couldn't be cuter. Buy pairs of different shaped pumpkins that can stack well on top of each other. Use black and white paint to create eyes and decorate the bottom pumpkin with patterns. Glue twigs to the side for arms and, voila: a new house pet.

# Pumpkin Oat Bars

A TASTY SNACK THAT'S HIGH ON ENERGY TO HELP LITTLE BODIES
THROUGH THE DAY, AND HIGH ON NUTRIENTS TO KEEP MUM HAPPY TOO

**SERVES 8**

1½ cups (130g, 4½ oz) quick oats

¼ cup (40g, 1½ oz) dark brown sugar

1 tsp baking powder

1 tsp ground cinnamon

½ tsp nutmeg

½ tsp salt

¼ cup (60ml, 2fl oz) milk

¼ cup (60ml, 2fl oz) thickened cream

1 large egg, beaten

1 tsp vanilla extract

1½ cups (340g, 12oz) cooked and mashed pumpkin

¼ cup (40g, 1½ oz) sultanas, chopped

¼ cup (30g, 1oz) pecans, chopped

Preheat the oven to 180°C (350°F, Gas Mark 4) and grease a 20 x 20cm (8 x 8in) baking tin.

Stir the oats, brown sugar, baking powder, cinnamon, nutmeg and salt together in a large mixing bowl. Make a well in the centre. Pour the milk, cream, egg and vanilla extract into the well and stir to combine. Add the pumpkin, sultanas and pecans and mix thoroughly. Pour the pumpkin batter into the prepared pan.

Bake in the oven for 25 minutes, or until a skewer inserted into the centre comes out clean. Cut into squares when cool.

# Pumpkin Pikelets

**MAKES 10**

2 eggs

1 cup (225g, 8oz) cooked and mashed pumpkin

½ cup (60g, 2oz) buckwheat (or plain) flour

¼ tsp vanilla essence

½ tsp baking powder

Pinch of cinnamon

Coconut oil or olive oil, for frying

Combine all the ingredients in a mixing bowl and whisk until a thick batter forms.

Heat oil in a frying pan over a medium-high heat.

Spoon the batter for one pikelet into the pan and cook for 2-3 minutes until golden brown, then flip and cook for 2-3 minutes on the other side. Repeat with the rest of the batter.

# Cottage Cheese Pancakes

**MAKES 8**

500g (1lb 2oz) cottage cheese

¾ cup (90g, 3oz) plain flour

5 eggs

½ tsp cinnamon

3 tbsps canola or vegetable oil

In a large bowl, mix together the cheese, flour, eggs and cinnamon.

Heat the oil in a large nonstick frying pan over medium heat.

Pour the batter into the frypan in ⅓ cup amounts.

Cook until bubbles appear on the surface of the pancakes.

Flip with a spatula and press down lightly to slightly flatten. The cakes are cooked once they are browned on both sides.

Serve with honey or maple syrup.

# COTTAGE CHEESE

This creamy, lumpy, light, zesty dairy spread is gentle on the mouth and tummy and super high in protein and calcium. It is great added as a dollop to all sorts of food that children love: peaches cut in quarters or a passionfruit cut in half, plain or scooped over honey on a salty cracker, mixed into a plate of scrambled eggs and lathered over toast. It's also an excellent addition to pancakes, perhaps swirled with strawberry jam.

# Sausage Rolls

WHY BUY PRE-MADE WHEN THIS VERSION CONTAINS JUST A FEW INGREDIENTS AND TAKES MINUTES TO PUT TOGETHER?

**MAKES 16**

2 sheets of frozen puff pastry

550g (1¼ lb) pork mince

1 onion, finely diced

1 carrot, finely grated

¼ cup (10g, ¼ oz) sage, chopped

1 egg, beaten with ½ cup (125ml, 4fl oz) milk

Sesame seeds

Preheat the oven to 180°C (350°F, Gas Mark 4).

Remove the puff pastry from the freezer and separate the pieces. Set aside to defrost for 10 minutes and then cut each sheet in half.

Mix the pork mince with the diced onion, carrot and sage.

Divide the mix into 4 even portions and spread in a line along each pastry rectangle.

Roll one edge of the pastry and tuck the sausage mix evenly under pastry.

Brush egg wash on the other edge and roll the pastry on top. Brush the top with egg wash and sprinkle with sesame seeds. Slice into 4 and place on an oven tray lined with baking paper.

Repeat until all the sausage mix is rolled and placed on trays.

Cook for around 25-20 minutes until pastry is golden brown.

# Chedder and Leek Mini Quiches

## THESE FLAVOUR-PACKED WONDERS WILL WIN OVER EVEN THE PICKIEST EATER IN THE FAMILY

**MAKES 24**

3 sheets frozen puff pastry, thawed

2 medium leeks, thinly sliced — white and light green parts only

2 tsps olive oil

⅔ cup (160ml, 5fl oz) cream

½ cup (60g, 2oz) Cheedar cheese, grated

¼ cup (30g, 1oz) Swiss cheese, grated

1 egg

1 egg yolk

1 tbsp fresh thyme leaves, chopped

½ tsp salt

¼ tsp pepper

Preheat oven to 200°C (400°F, Gas Mark 6). Lightly oil two 12-hole muffin tins.

Cut the sheets of pastry into rounds that will fit snugly into the muffin holes, coming up to the edges of each one. Re-roll out the spare pastry if you need more circles. Gently push each circle into a muffin hole.

In a medium frying pan over medium-high heat saute the leeks in olive oil until softened, but don't let them brown. Let them cool slightly.

In a large bowl, add the cream, cheeses, egg, egg yolk, thyme, salt and pepper. Mix thoroughly, then add the leek to the mixture and stir to combine.

Place one dessertspoon of the mixture into each lined muffin hole.

Place in the preheated oven and bake for 20 minutes, until the crusts and tops are golden brown.

# Pizza Rolls

TURN YOUR BACK AND THEY'RE GONE! MAKE PLENTY BECAUSE THESE OOZY, STICKY, CHEESY PIZZA ROLLS WON'T LAST LONG

**MAKES 10**

### DOUGH

2 cups (250g, 8oz) self-raising flour

Pinch of salt

90g (3oz) butter, chopped

²/₃ cup (160ml, 5fl oz) milk

1 cup (250ml, 8fl oz) pizza or pasta sauce

2 cups (250g, 8oz) mozzarella, shredded

½ cup (60g, 2oz) Parmesan, finely grated

1 tsp dried oregano

10 slices Virginia ham

Pinch of chilli flakes (optional)

Preheat oven to 190°C (375°F, Gas Mark 5). Line a baking tray with baking paper.

Sift the flour and salt into a mixing bowl. Add the butter and rub it into the flour with your fingertips until a rough crumble forms.

Make a well in the centre and start to gradually add the milk. Mix lightly with your hands to bring the mixture together. Add more milk if needed until a soft, sticky dough forms.

Knead the dough on a clean, dry and lightly floured surface until smooth. Roll out the dough to form a rectangle, then cut it crosswise into 4 smaller rectangles. Dust pizza dough with flour if needed.

Spread a thin layer of pizza sauce over each rectangle, leaving a 2cm (1in) border along one short side. Sprinkle cheeses and oregano over each piece and top with ham.

Roll up each rectangle, starting with one short side. Press the edges together to seal. Repeat with the remaining dough. Cut each roll into 2cm (1in) slices using a sharp knife.

Place the rolls on the prepared baking tray and transfer to the oven to bake for 15-20 minutes or until cheese has melted and the edges are golden brown. Serve warm out of the oven for maximum gooeyness.

# Bolognese Bake

## A GREAT WAY TO SERVE PASTA AND BOLOGNAISE THAT ALLOWS YOU TIME TO SET THE TABLE WHILE IT'S FINISHING OFF IN THE OVEN

**SERVES 4**

2 tbsps olive oil

500g (1lb 2oz) beef mince

1 onion, finely chopped

3 cloves garlic, chopped

2 x 400g (14oz) cans crushed tomatoes

½ cup (125ml, 4fl oz) tomato paste

2 tsps fresh oregano, chopped, or 1 tsp dried oregano

½ bunch fresh parsley, chopped

Salt and pepper, to taste

300g (10oz) penne

¼ cup (30g, 1oz) tasty cheese, grated

¼ cup (30g, 1oz) pecorino or Parmesan cheese, grated

Parsley, to garnish

Preheat the oven to 180°C (350°F, Gas Mark 4).

Heat 1 tablespoon of the oil in a large frying pan over medium-high heat. Add the mince and fry for 6-8 minutes, stirring, until fully browned with no sign of pink meat. Drain and set aside.

Heat the remaining oil in the same pan. Saute the onions until soft and lightly golden. Add the garlic and fry for a further minute.

Add the tomatoes, tomato paste, oregano and parsley and return meat to the pan. Bring the sauce to a boil. Taste and season with salt and pepper as needed. Reduce heat to low and gently simmer for 15 minutes.

Meanwhile, cook the penne according to the packet instructions and drain.

In a large bowl, mix bolognese sauce together with the pasta and transfer to a medium-sized baking dish. Sprinkle with cheese and bake in the oven for 20 minutes until the cheese is bubbling. Remove from the oven and allow to cool. Garnish with parsley and serve.

**NOTE:** This bake can be sliced up when cold, wrapped in foil and added to a lunchbox.

# Low-Sugar Sweets

# APPLES

Apples are an all day, every day fruit. They're an amazing snack straight from mother nature — bitten into and chewed to the core. The skin is pumping with the antioxidant quercetin and the white, delicious flesh of apples is full of fibre. Apples are super versatile to cook with — bake, steam, stew, saute, fry, or cover in caramel to transform them into giant lollipops. And they're also an excellent teaching treat: taking the kids to an apple orchard is a fun trip and will get them thinking how sweet it is that one of their favourite foods comes from trees.

## CLASSIC APPLE VARIETIES

RED DELICIOUS: Mild in flavour — tastes almost like apple juice without the sugar. These classic apples are hydrating and refreshing and great for children who are not super adventurous eaters. The flavour can get lost when baking but they're good for tossing into salads or cutting into quarters and snacking.

GOLDEN DELICIOUS: They taste just as they sound, delicious and sunny — perfect chopped into cubes for a picnic, maybe drizzled in honey or tossed with slices of strawberry. They are sweet and not tart. They are a favourite for baking in pies or warming up and plonking on the table for dessert with some ice cream.

PINK LADY: Sweet and very juicy. They taste a bit tropical, with hints of pineapple and banana in there. These are excellent for eating and baking.

JONATHAN: Yummier than a glass of juice. These are designed to be held by little hands — small and red with subtle streaks of bright lime, Jonathans are firm and very crunchy, so the only thing to be careful of is those loose teeth waiting to break free.

GALA: Mildly sweet and a little bit tender in texture. Gala are a touch chewy and sometimes, they give that tart, tongue-smacking after taste. These are better for eating than baking.

## A HEALTHY TOFFEE APPLE

How luxurious is a toffee apple — heavy and sweet, crunchy and juicy. And yet, toffee can wreak havoc on little teeth and lead to sugar highs and then lows.

SOLUTION: Buy a punnet or a bag of pitted medjool dates — these chewy fruits taste like brown sugar naturally. Throw them in a blender with coconut oil, lemon juice, salt and vanilla extract and blend until it's thick and smooth. Poke sticks into Golden Delicious apples and roll them around in the natural caramel mixture. Top with coconut or almonds and this is almost too healthy.

# Avocado Apple Smoothie

**SERVES 2**

1 banana (fresh or frozen)

1 cup (250ml, 8fl oz) coconut milk

2 dates, pitted

1 apple, peeled and cored

1 avocado, peeled and pitted

1 tsp vanilla extract

½ cup (75g, 3oz) ice cubes

Cacao nibs, to garnish (optional)

Add all the ingredients except the garnish to the blender and process until smooth enough to drink.

Pour into glasses, top with cacao nibs, if using, and serve immediately.

# Easy Apple Muffins

**MAKES 12**

2½ cups (310g, 10oz) plain flour

1 tbsp baking powder

1½ tsps ground cinnamon

1 cup (155g, 5oz) brown sugar, firmly packed

2 medium apples, peeled and roughly chopped

¾ cup (120g, 4oz) raisins

125g (4oz) butter, melted, cooled

2 eggs, lightly whisked

¾ cup (185ml, 6fl oz) milk

Preheat oven to 200°C (390°F, Gas Mark 6) and line a 12-hole muffin tray with muffin cases.

Sift flour, baking powder and cinnamon together into a large bowl. Stir in brown sugar, apples and raisins and mix until well combined. Whisk the butter, eggs and milk with a hand whisk until well combined. Add the wet ingredients to the dry ingredients and stir with a large metal spoon until just combined. Do not over-mix.

Spoon the mixture evenly into the muffin cases. Place in the oven and bake the muffins for 20 minutes or until golden and a skewer comes out clean.

# CINNAMON

Cinnamon toast is one of the best treats of childhood and when the bread is whole wheat or multigrain, spread with almond butter and then sprinkled lightly in cinnamon — no sugar — there's nothing more fun and yummy to snack on. It gets better: mash a banana with a teaspoon of cinnamon and spread that over bread or dip rice crackers into it as though it's hummus. Or just sprinkle on some crisp apples for a yummy snack. Cinnamon has antioxidant qualities and is great for the immune system.

# Mini Apple Tarts

TOO EASY — YOU CAN HAVE THESE LITTLE TREATS IN THE OVEN IN UNDER TEN MINUTES

**MAKES 12**

55g (2oz) unsalted butter

4 sheets puff pastry

4 large apples, such as sundowner or pink lady, peeled, cored, and finely chopped

¼ cup (60ml, 2fl oz) orange juice, freshly squeezed (or just use water)

2 tbsps brown sugar (optional)

1 tbsp cornflour

1 tsp vanilla extract

1 tsp cinnamon

Preheat the oven to 180°C (350°F, Gas Mark 4).

Melt half of the butter and use it to lightly grease the muffin holes of a 12-hole muffin tin.

Lay out the sheets of puff pastry and cut out 12 circles. It's easiest to use a biscuit cutter, or you can improvise with the base of a glass bottle. Gently press each circle of pastry into the muffin pan, creating your bowl for the apple filling.

In a medium-sized bowl, combine apples, juice, sugar, if using, cornflour, vanilla and cinnamon. Make sure the mixture is well combined.

Using a spoon, fill up each tart shell equally with the apple filling. The mixture will reduce while it cooks so it's okay if you have heaped the mix quite high.

Top each mini tart with a ¼ teaspoon of the remaining butter.

Place in the oven and bake for 30 minutes or until the pastry and top of the tart filling is browned. Take out of the oven and let cool in the tin for about 10-15 minutes.

Serve warm.

# Glazed Oatmeal Cookies

THESE SWEET COOKIES HAVE A WHOLESOME VIBE THAT'S A GOOD LOOK FOR LUNCHBOXES AND WILL KEEP THE KIDS ENERGY LEVELS UP

**MAKES 20**

⅔ cup (100g, 3½ oz) raisins

⅔ cup (160ml, 5fl oz) coconut oil

1 cup (220g, 8oz) raw (or brown) sugar

1 egg, beaten

1 tsp ground cinnamon

1 tsp vanilla extract

1¼ cups (155g, 5oz) whole wheat flour

¼ tsp bicarbonate of soda

Pinch of salt

150g (5oz) oats

### GLAZE

1 cup (155g, 5oz) icing sugar

1 tsp cinnamon

2 tbsps milk

¼ tsp vanilla extract

Heat the oven to 180°C (350°F, Gas Mark 4) and line a shallow-sided baking tray (you may need two) with greaseproof paper.

Just cover the raisins with boiling water and leave to soak for 20 minutes until plump. Drain, reserving the liquid.

In a large bowl, mix together oil and sugar. Gradually beat in the egg and then add cinnamon, vanilla extract and the water from the raisins. Sift the flour, bicarb and salt into the bowl. Add the oats and stir. Finally, mix in the raisins and stir until well combined.

Scrape the dough into the baking tray. Bake for 15 minutes until golden. Leave to cool in the tray for 10 minutes then transfer to a wire rack to cool completely. When cool slice into desired shapes.

When cookies are cool, whisk together the ingredients for the glaze and swirl or spread it on top of the cookies. If you need to adjust the consistency of the glaze, add more icing sugar for thickness or more milk to thin it down.

Store in an airtight container for up to 3 days.

# Mango Coconut Slice

KNOWN AS 'BARFI' IN INDIA. THIS SIMPLE SLICE IS A DELICIOUS SWEET TREAT THAT THE WHOLE FAMILY CAN ENJOY

**MAKES 12**

1 large or 2 small mangos, peeled and seeded

½ cup (40g, 1½ oz) desiccated coconut

½ cup (125ml, 4fl oz) milk

½ cup (110g, 4oz) Natvia (see page 129)

Handful of pistachio nuts, roughly chopped

First, puree the mango flesh by blitzing it in a food processor or high-speed blender. Set aside.

Butter a square or rectangular shallow-sided dish.

Place the desiccated coconut in a large frying pan over a medium heat and cook for 1-2 minutes, stirring occasionally, until lightly toasted.

Add the milk, Natvia and mango puree and cook, stirring frequently, for up to 20 minutes until the mixture has dried out but is still sticky enough to hold together.

Transfer the mixture to the baking tray and press into the tray. Place the pistachio nuts on top and gently press them into the slice.

Cover with plastic wrap and transfer to the fridge to chill. Remove from the fridge about 20 minutes prior to serving and slice into squares.

# Walnut and Raisin Cookies

## A FRESH TAKE ON FRUIT-AND-NUT COOKIES THAT'S CHEWY, TASTY AND FULL OF NUTRITIOUS INGREDIENTS

**MAKES 10**

⅔ cup (100g, 3½ oz) raisins

1 tbsp ground chia seeds

½ cup (125ml, 4fl oz) coconut oil, soft

⅓ cup cup (70g, 2½ oz) coconut sugar

1 tsp pure vanilla extract

¼ tsp salt

½ tsp bicarbonate of soda

1 cup (125g, 4oz) oat flour

Pinch of salt

½ cup (40g, 1½ oz) oats

½ cup (60g, 2oz) walnuts, finely chopped

Heat the oven to 180°C (350°F, Gas Mark 4) and line a baking tray with greaseproof paper.

Cover the raisins with boiling water and leave to soak for 20 mins until plump. Drain and set aside.

Place the chia seeds in a small bowl. Add 3 tablespoons of water and set aside to soak for 20 minutes until a gel forms.

In a medium mixing bowl, cream together the coconut oil and coconut sugar until well combined. Add the vanilla extract, salt, and chia seed gel and mix everything together.

Add the bicarb, oat flour, pinch of salt and oats and mix until combined. Fold in the walnuts and raisins.

Drop heaped tablespoons of the dough onto the baking tray, and using your hands shape to the desired shape and thickness. Bake for 15 minutes until golden and the centre is just set. Leave to cool on the tray for 10 minutes then transfer to a wire rack to cool completely.

Store in an airtight container for up to 3 days.

# WHY LOW SUGAR?

Why avoid refined white sugar? Excessive sugar consumption can cause type 2 diabetes and obesity, both big problems in the Western world. It's the fructose molecule found in refined sugar (and other sugars) that's to blame. The body can't process too much fructose, and it quickly turns to fat in the liver, causing diabetes, heart disease and other health problems. Glucose, on the other hand, is metabolised by all the cells in our body. The average Australian, Brit or American consumes in the region of 27 teaspoons of sugar a day, but the World Health Organization recommends just 6 teaspoons. There are plenty of sugar substitutes and sweeteners on the market these days, so how do you choose?

STEVIA: Stevia is a natural herb that is processed for use in cooking as a powder or liquid. It's very sweet, but it is 100% fructose free. One teaspoon of liquid stevia equates to one tablespoon of powdered stevia which equals a cup of old-fashioned sugar.

ERYTHRITOL: Despite it's scientific-sounding name, erythritol is a naturally occurring nectar in plants, and fruits and vegetables like grapes and mushrooms. It's a good choice when looking for a direct substitute for sugar as it measures the same cup for cup.

NATVIA: Natvia is a natural sweetener made by combining the purest and sweetest parts of the stevia plant and erythritol. Natvia is fructose free. It can be used as a direct substitute for sugar.

COCONUT SUGAR: A sustainable option made from the sap of the coconut palm, it is nutritious and has a low GI, which means no sugar high and lows. Can be used as a direct substitute for sugar.

MAPLE SYRUP: The sugary sap from the maple tree is delicious, but it contains about 40% fructose, so use in moderation. Maple syrup can replace regular sugar as and when you need it.

HONEY: Honey is made up of around 75% sugar (glucose and fructose equally). It has more calories than sugar but because it's sweeter you can use less of it. Choose honey that's been organically produced to reap the full benefits, such as antioxidant and antibacterial properties.

RICE MALT SYRUP (ALSO KNOWN AS BROWN RICE SYRUP): Made from boiling brown rice, this syrup is gluten and wheat free. It has a mild butterscotch flavour and can be used as a condiment as well as a sugar substitute in cooking. It is 100% fructose free. It can be used as a direct substitute for sugar or honey.

# Blueberry Cake

QUICK AND EASY, THIS MOIST LOAF CAKE IS A SURE-FIRE SUCCESS FOR THE KIDS' LUNCHBOXES

**SERVES 6**

2 cups (250g, 8oz) plain flour

2 tsps baking powder

½ tsp salt

2 egg whites

2 tbsps coconut oil (or butter)

½ tsp vanilla extract

½ cup (180g, 6oz) rice malt syrup

½ cup (125ml, 4fl oz) Greek yoghurt

¼ cup (60ml, 2fl oz) milk

2 cups (200g, 7oz) blueberries, fresh or frozen

Preheat the oven to 190°C (375°F, Gas Mark 5). Line a 20 x 10 x 7cm (8 x 4 x 3in) loaf tin with greaseproof paper.

Sift the flour, baking powder and salt in a large mixing bowl. In a separate bowl, mix together the egg white, coconut oil and vanilla. Add the rice malt syrup, yoghurt and milk and stir everything together quickly. Pour the wet ingredients into the bowl containing the dry ingredients. Add the blueberries. Using a large wooden spoon, gently fold together until all the mixture is wet.

Pour into the prepared tin and bake for 35-45 minutes until a skewer inserted in the centre comes out clean. Cut and serve warm or cold.

# Dried Fruit Bars

## THESE HEALTHY AND NUTRITIOUS BARS ARE THE PERFECT PICK-ME-UP FOR EVERY ON-THE-GO FAMILY MEMBER

**MAKES 12**

½ cup (20g, ¾ oz) bran flakes

½ cup (125g, 4oz) peanut butter

¼ cup (90g, 3oz) maple syrup

Pinch of salt

⅓ cup (80ml, 3fl oz) water

⅓ cup (50g, 2oz) chopped dates

¼ cup (40g, 1½ oz) chopped cranberries

¼ cup (40g, 1½ oz) chopped raisins

⅓ cup (40g, 1½ oz) almonds

¼ cup (30g, 1oz) chopped pecans

¼ cup (30g, 1oz) chopped hazelnuts

Preheat oven to 165°C (330°F, Gas Mark 3).

Place all ingredients into a blender and blend until the mixture begins to clump together.

Line an 18 x 28cm (7 x 11in) slice tin with baking paper and press the mix into the tin.

Bake for 30 minutes until top is dry and edges are a deep, toasted brown.

Cut into long rectangles.

Once they have cooled completely, you can store them in an airtight container for around 2 weeks.

# Cheat's Berry Ice Cream

**SERVES 6**

300g (10oz) frozen blueberries

3 tbsps honey

½ tsp vanilla extract

1¼ cups (285ml, 10fl oz) extra-thick double cream

Place the blueberries, honey and vanilla extract into a food processor. Blitz for 5 seconds until a pulp forms. Add the cream and blitz again for 10 seconds.

Spoon into dishes and serve immediately.

**NOTE:** You can also transfer to the freezer to chill for 30 minuts for a semi-frozen version of this dish.

# Yoghurt Berry Cereal Pops

**MAKES 6**

**BERRY SYRUP**

1 cup (100g, 3½ oz) blueberries

½ cup (60g, 2oz) raspberries

3 tbsps maple syrup

**POPSICLES**

1½ cups (240g, 12oz) plain Greek yohgurt

¾ cup (185ml, 6fl oz) milk

1 tbsp maple syrup

¾ cup (120g, 4oz) granola (retaining some to finish)

Bring berries and maple syrup to a boil in a saucepan over high heat. Reduce to a simmer and cook, stirring, for 10 minutes.

Mix yoghurt, milk, maple syrup and granola in a bowl. Pour over berry syrup and leave for 2 minutes to loosely combine.

Pour mixture into moulds, ending with a sprinkle of granola. Insert sticks and freeze overnight.

# Healthy Beet Balls

**MAKES 15**

150g (5oz) beetroot, peeled

65g (2oz) dates

½ cup (60g, 2oz) macadamia nuts

¼ cup (60ml, 2fl oz) coconut oil

¼ cup (50g, 2oz) cacao butter

¼ cup (20g, ¾ oz) desiccated coconut

½ tsp vanilla extract

¼ cup (60ml, 2fl oz) maple syrup

Water, as needed

In a food processor, blend all of the ingredients until well combined.

Add a spoonful of water at a time until mixture is desired texture.

Using hands, roll bite-sized balls from the mixture.

Serve immediately, or store in the fridge.

# Beetroot and Apple Juice

**SERVES 2**

2 cups (500ml, 1pt) coconut water

2 stalks celery

1 large beetroot, peeled

2 apples, peeled and cored

Pour all the ingredients through a juicer. Discard the pulp and serve immediately.

**NOTE:** If you don't have a juicer, use a blender. Simply strain through a fine mesh sieve or cheesecloth.

# BEETROOT

The best thing about beetroot is its colour — it's redder than any lolly out there and when eaten raw, as crunchy as an apple. Raw beetroot has a mild earthy taste with a hint of fruity sweet. When roasted or sauteed, it's as soft and sweet on little tongues as a raspberry. Kids love to behold a bright purple-red milkshake or juice, which is bursting with folic acid, fibre and vitamin C that will help those cheeks flush. And toddlers have fun in the mirror with stained lips. (Tip: lemon juice is a great remover.)

# Mango and Coconut Balls

EASY, EASY, EASY, THESE LITTLE BITES OF TROPICAL PARADISE CAN BE MADE IN MINUTES AND STORED IN THE FRIDGE TO EAT LATER

**MAKES 15**

150g (5oz) dried mango

½ cup (60g, 2oz) macadamia nuts

¼ cup (60ml, 2fl oz) coconut oil

¼ cup (50g, 2oz) cacao butter

¼ cup (20g, ¾oz) desiccated coconut

½ tsp vanilla extract

¼ cup (60ml, 2fl oz) maple syrup

Water, as needed

In a food processor, blend together the mango, macadamia nuts, coconut oil, cacao butter, coconut, vanilla extract and maple syrup until well combined and a thick paste has formed.

Add a spoonful of water at a time until mixture is desired texture. It needs to be sticky enough to hold together but dry enough to roll into balls so that it won't stick to your hands. Test the mixture as you go.

Using hands, roll bite-sized balls from the mixture.

Serve immediately, or store in fridge.

# Hulk Balls

A DASH OF MATCHA POWDER WILL TURN THESE BALLS A BRIGHT GREEN AND MAKE SUPERHEROES OF YOUR LITTLE ONES

**MAKES 15**

¾ cup (90g, 3oz) cashew nuts

¼ cup pistachio nuts, shelled

2 tbsps ground flaxseed

½ cup (80g, 3oz) dried cranberries

¾ cup (130g, 4oz) Medjool dates, pitted

1 tbsp coconut oil

½ cup (40g, 1½ oz) desiccated coconut

2 tsps matcha powder

Place the cashew nuts, pistachios and flaxseed in a food processor. Blitz for 1 minute, until roughly chopped.

Add the cranberries, dates, coconut oil, desiccated coconut and matcha powder and blend for a further 1 minute until a dough forms.

Using hands, form the mixture into little balls.

Store in an airtight container in the fridge or freezer.

# Energy Balls

SWEET, RICH AND CHOCOLATEY, THIS RECIPE PROVIDES A GREAT
WAY TO INTRODUCE ENERGY BALLS TO THE KIDS

**MAKES 15**

12 pitted dates

1 tbsp cacao powder

2 tbsps cacao butter (or
use peanut butter)

¾ cup (90g, 3oz)
walnuts

½ cup (40g, 1½ oz)
desiccated coconut

1-2 tbsps honey, to
taste

Place the dates, cacao powder and butter in a high-speed blender
or food processor and process until a thick paste forms.

Add the walnuts and coconut and pulse until the desired
consistency is achieved.

Add honey in small quantities, pulsing in between. Taste and add
more to achieve desired sweetness.

Using damp hands, roll into balls of the desired size and place on
a tray lined with baking paper.

Place in the fridge until set, then transfer to an airtight container
and store in the fridge up to 1 week.

**NOTE:** Consider adding grated fresh ginger for a version of these
balls that has a little kick to it — a great after-dinner chocolate.

# Everyday Banana Loaf

AN EASY STAPLE FOR THE FAMILY TO SNACK ON, THIS VERSION IS SWEETENED BY DATES SO IT'S LOW FRUCTOSE TOO

**SERVES 6**

3 bananas, medium ripe, mashed

2 tbsps rice malt syrup

65g (2oz) pitted dates, chopped

1 egg, beaten

1 cup (125g, 4oz) self-raising flour, sifted

Pinch of salt

2 tbsps sesame seeds, to top

Preheat oven to 180°C (350°F, Gas Mark 4) and line the base of a standard loaf tin with baking paper.

Mash the bananas with a fork in a large mixing bowl. Add the golden syrup and stir to combine. Stir in the dates and mix everything together thoroughly.

In a separate bowl, whisk together the egg, flour and salt until just combined into a batter. Scrape the batter into the bowl with the bananas and stir well to incorporate.

Pour mixture into the loaf tin and sprinkle with sesame seeds.

Transfer to the oven to bake for 30 minutes or until a skewer inserted in the centre comes out clean.

# CACAO

Cacao is bursting with iron, protein, and magnesium, which are all energy boosting and also tend to make big and little people smilier after eating — both from the taste and from cacao's almost magical health properties.

## WHAT IS CACAO?

It's not cocoa but it does come from the same tree, the cacao tree. Cacao is very similar to cocoa, only healthier. So in some sense, when explaining it to a young one, it could be said that cacao is basically chocolate. And if their eyes widen, slip in that it is the purest form of chocolate.

Cacao is chocolate before any chocolate company has gotten its hands and machines on it. It is the seed of a small reddish-brown fruit, less processed than cocoa and so has retained all the original vitamins and minerals from the plant. (Cocoa powder is raw cacao that's been roasted at high temperatures, losing some of its nutritional potency.) There is no fat in there either.

Cacao contains antioxidants known as flavonoids — they are also found in tea and red wine and are healthy for the heart and for reducing inflammation. Inflammation is a bit of an 'it' word these days, as studies suggest that processed, refined and sugary foods can cause inflammation inside and out, which can lead to many diseases, including heart disease and diabetes.

## HOW TO EAT IT

Is there any child who needs more reason to eat chocolate? Well, it can take a little time for chocolate lovers — children and older! — to become cacao addicts but there are lots of baby steps to get there.

Cacao comes in 'nibs', which are little nuggets or solid flakes — as though someone fed a block of chocolate through a shredder. Eat it straight from the pack or add it to trail mix for a big day out. The nibs are a treat in muesli or granola. They are lightly crunchy and are rich like chocolate but not sweet. If any convincing is needed, start adding them to desserts and treats that are usually sweet. The kids will start to associate the taste of cacao with the taste of, say, ice cream. Eventually, maybe they won't even want the ice cream. Cacao and honey also go great together in a smoothie with almond milk and Greek yoghurt — it's grainy and creamy, sweet and salty.

Cacao also comes as a powder that can be easily stirred into drinks and baking mixes to add a chocolatey texture and taste. Try a recipe like rich chocolate cake with cacao or triple chocolate biscuits and see if the children even notice.

# Easy Beetroot Brownie

SNEAKING BEETROOT INTO BROWNIES IS A CRAFTY MUM TRICK —
AND IT'S EASY, AS YOU'LL FIND OUT IF YOU TRY THIS RECIPE

**SERVES 8**

250g (9oz) dark
chocolate, chopped

250g (9oz) butter,
cut into cubes

1½ cups (250g, 9oz)
beetroot, cooked

3 eggs

1 tsp vanilla essence

1 cup (220g, 8oz)
coconut sugar

¼ cup (30g, 1oz)
cocoa or cacao powder

½ cup (60g, 2oz) rice
flour (or plain flour)

1 tsp baking powder

1 cup (100g, 3½ oz)
almond meal

Icing sugar, for dusting

Preheat oven to 180°C (350°F, Gas Mark 4). Line a rectangular
tin with greaseproof paper.

Melt chocolate and butter in a heatproof bowl placed over a pan
of simmering water.

Place cooked beetroot in a food processor and pulse until
pureed. Add the eggs one at a time, followed by the vanilla and
coconut sugar, and mix until smooth.

Sift cocoa powder, rice flour and baking powder into a bowl
and stir in almond meal. Stir beetroot mixture into the melted
chocolate and then fold in the dry ingredients.

Pour the mixture into the tin and bake in the oven for 30
minutes, until just firm to the touch and a skewer inserted in the
centre comes out slightly sticky. Leave to cool in the tin and then
cut into squares. Dust with icing sugar before serving.

# Spiced Choc 'n' Nut Slice

## A CHRISTMAS SPECIAL THAT'S GREAT FOR THE FAMILY TO ENJOY AT ANY TIME OF YEAR

**SERVES 8**

5 tbsps unsweetened cocoa or cacao powder

2½ cups (325g, 11oz) hazelnuts

1 cup (125g, 4oz) plain flour

1 cup (170g, 6oz) mixed dried fruit

1 tbsp ground cinnamon

2 tsps ground ginger

Pinch of grated nutmeg

90g (3oz) dark chocolate, chopped

½ cup (220g, 8oz) coconut sugar

¾ cup (260g, 9oz) maple syrup (or honey)

Icing sugar, for dusting

Preheat the oven to 160°C (325°F, Gas Mark 3) and grease and line a large baking tin. Dust the inside (base and sides) with cocoa powder.

In a large bowl, mix together the cocoa powder, nuts, flour, dried fruit, cinnamon, ginger and nutmeg.

Melt the chocolate in a small heatproof bowl set over a pan of simmering water. Set aside when just melted.

Heat the coconut sugar and maple syrup in a saucepan over a medium-high heat until completely dissolved and the syrup has thickened.

Pour the hot syrup over the nut mixture. Add the melted chocolate, and stir to combine.

Scrape the batter into the prepared tin and carefully smooth the surface with a spatula.

Transfer to the oven and bake for 40 minutes until set but still just soft in the centre.

Transfer to a wire rack to cool for 15 minutes, then remove from the tin to cool completely. Cut into squares when cool.

Dust with icing sugar to serve.

# School-Night Dinners

# FINGER FOOD

Rules are important and they're much easier to follow if there are plenty of special occasions for breaking them. Finger food is of course one of the all time best reasons to have a birthday party. It doesn't have to be just once a year, though. How about one night a week of doing away with the knife and fork and setting a challenge: everyone in the family come up with new healthy recipes for finger food night. And there's no need to set the table.

## GUILT-FREE FINGER FOODS

HALLOUMI AND FRUIT: The chewy white cheese is a fun source of salty protein. It looks and tastes amazing cut into rectangles, grilled or barbecued and laid on a platter with peaches or nectarines or mangoes cut into quarters. The sugar of the fruit mellows the salt of the cheese.

FRIES THAT AREN'T FRIES: Naughty, greasy hot chips have evolved in a big way in recent years and so 'fries' is no longer a dirty word in healthy households. The humble potato is great when lathered in olive oil and baked, rather than fried. And substitute this for an array of vegetables and grains that can be cut into finger shapes and eaten slow or gobbled. Try pre-cooked polenta from the fridge section in the supermarket, seasoned and served with a chunky fresh tomato dip. Experiment with veggies: sweet potato, carrots, green beans, pumpkin, zucchini and asparagus are just for starters. All can be seasoned with salt, pepper, Parmesan cheese and perhaps some rosemary.

SAUCES: Finger food is for dipping. There are so many healthy sauces that can be made with light, nutritious bases like tomatoes, yoghurt or cottage cheese. Hummus is also an excellent dipping alternative. Add vegetable puree or seasoning to hummus and you have dipping snacks for a week.

CHICKEN AND FISH FINGERS: these are a healthy treat when home-made. Start with chicken strips or a light, white fish. Lightly bread them in polenta or a nut flour, which delivers protein and vitamins along with the fried crunch, and bake in the oven.

STRAWBERRIES DIPPED IN CHOCOLATE: These are delicious freshly made. Use dark or white cooking chocolate and get the kids poking strawberries with skewers, and then swirling in the velvety melted chocolate. For extra oomph, stick them in the freezer — they taste like summer.

FROZEN BANANA ICE CREAMS: Dark chocolate is the obvious dipping choice for these creamy, cold treats, or try caramel sauce for a gentler, equally gorgeous sweet dessert.

# Grilled Chicken Sesame Kebabs with Sesame Sauce

THESE TASTY MEATBALLS ARE A GENTLE WAY TO INTRODUCE ASIAN FLAVOURS TO LITTLE PEOPLE — LEAVE THE SAUCE OFF IF IT'S TOO MUCH

**MAKES 8**

### MEATBALLS

700g (1½ lb) chicken mince

½ cup (60g, 2oz) breadcrumbs

2 spring onions, finely chopped

1 egg, beaten

2 tsps fresh ginger, peeled and finely grated

2 cloves garlic, peeled and crushed

1 tsp toasted sesame oil

1 tsp salt

8-10 small wooden skewers, soaked in warm water for at least 30 minutes to prevent burning and the wood from splintering

### SESAME SAUCE

¼ cup (60ml, 2fl oz) soy sauce

1 clove garlic, peeled and crushed

2 tbsps seasoned rice wine vinegar

1 tbsp maple syrup

½ tsp fresh ginger, peeled and finely grated

2 tsps sesame oil

½ tbsp fresh lime juice

1 tsp toasted sesame seeds, to garnish

### SAUCE

Combine the soy sauce, garlic, vinegar, maple syrup, ginger, sesame oil and lime juice to make the sauce marinade.

### KEBABS

In a bowl, mix the chicken, breadcrumbs, spring onions, egg, ginger, garlic, sesame oil and salt. Use your hands to mix thoroughly and then shape into small meatballs, using about 1 dessertspoon of mixture for each. Thread 3 meatballs onto each skewer.

Heat a grill pan (or barbecue grill) to high heat. Carefully place the skewers onto the grill, taking care that the mix doesn't fall off the skewers. Cook each skewer on one side first for 4 minutes, then gently turn over and cook for 2 minutes on the other three sides. The kebabs should be well browned all over and cooked all the way through.

Remove from grill pan and sprinkle over the toasted sesame seeds. Drizzle with the sauce and serve.

# Chicken Pumpkin Kebab

## MOIST, SWEET AND LITTLE BIT SPICY THESE TASTY KEBABS BRIGHTEN UP ANY DINNER PLATE

**MAKES 12**

¼ cup (40g, 1½ oz) brown sugar

¼ cup (60ml, 2fl oz) orange juice

¼ cup (60ml, 2fl oz) soy sauce

1 tsp fresh ginger, minced

1 tsp sesame oil

1 tsp chilli powder

500g (1lb 2oz) chicken breasts, cut into 3cm (1in) cubes

1kg (2lb) butternut pumpkin, cut into 3cm (1in) cubes

2 tbsps olive oil

Sea salt, to taste

6 small onions, quartered

12 wooden skewers, soaked in hot water for at least an hour.

2 tbsps flat-leaf parsley, finely chopped, to garnish

Preheat oven to 190°C (375°F, Gas Mark 5).

In a medium-sized jar, combine the sugar, juice, soy sauce, ginger, sesame oil and chilli powder. Close the jar and shake to mix thoroughly to create the marinade.

In a medium bowl, combine the chicken breast pieces with half of the marinade. Set aside and let the chicken soak for at least 1 hour.

In the meantime, line a baking tray with baking paper. Place the cubed pumpkin pieces on the sheet and drizzle over the olive oil and sprinkle with salt. Bake in the preheated oven for 20 minutes, until the pumpkin is just tender. It needs to still be slightly firm so it can be threaded onto the skewers.

Thread the pumpkin cubes, chicken pieces and a couple of wedges of onion onto the skewers in whatever order you like. Use up all the ingredients until the pieces are evenly spread among the skewers.

Heat a grill pan or barbecue grill to high heat. Place the skewers onto the grill, and  cook each skewer on one side first for 4 minutes, then gently turn over and cook for 2 minutes on the other three sides. Drizzle over small amounts of the marinade as you cook, to keep them moist.

The kebabs should be well browned all over and cooked all the way through. Serve warm and sprinkle over the chopped parsley.

# Easy BBQ Sauce

**MAKES 3 CUPS**

2 cups (450g, 1lb) tomato sauce

¼ cup (90g, 3oz) honey

¼ cup (40g, 1½ oz) brown sugar

½ cup (125ml, 4fl oz) apple cider vinegar

¾ cup (185ml, 6fl oz) water

1 tsp freshly ground pepper

1 tbsp lemon juice

1 tbsp Worcestershire sauce

Place all the ingredients in a saucepan over a medium-high heat and bring to the boil, stirring constantly. Reduce the heat to a gentle simmer and cook, uncovered, for 45 minutes. Stir occasionally. If the mixture appears too thick, add a little more water. If it is too thin, increase the heat slightly and/or cook for an additional period of time until the desired consistency has been reached.

Remove from the heat and set aside to cool. Transfer to a jar and store in the fridge for up to 2 weeks.

# Sweet Chilli Sauce

**MAKES 2 CUPS**

10 red bird's-eye chillies, roughly chopped

½ x 400g (14oz) can diced tomatoes

¼ cup (55g, 2oz) sugar

¼ cup (60ml, 2fl oz) white wine vinegar

Bring chillies, tomatoes, sugar and vinegar to the boil in a saucepan over high heat.

Reduce heat and simmer for 5-10 minutes, until sauce thickens.

Remove from heat and set aside for 5 minutes.

In a blender, process the mixture in batches until smooth.

If not using immediately, pour into hot sterilised jars with secure lids.

# GRILLED FRUIT

How exciting as a new chef to discover that a pineapple is not just a pineapple. This is especially true when it is thrown in slices on to the barbecue or grill where it gathers a rich, salty flavour from the heat and its texture becomes both lighter and sticky like caramel. Do this with most fruits — peaches grill especially well, as do apples and bananas — and the kids will think the fruit salad is straight from the 'treats' aisle. Toss in some mint and scoop over creamy Greek yoghurt and it's a family affair.

# Pizza Verde on Cauliflower Crust

CAULIFLOWER CRUST? IT MIGHT NOT BE PIZZA DOUGH AS YOU KNOW IT BUT IT TASTES REALLY GOOD IN A NUTTY, EARTHY KIND OF A WAY

**SERVES 4**

### CRUST

1 large head cauliflower, cut into chunks

200g (7 oz) almond meal

3 eggs, beaten

2 tbsps dried mixed herbs

½ tsp salt

¼ tsp pepper

### TOMATO SAUCE

2 x 225g (8oz) cans tomato paste

2 tbsps olive oil

2 cloves garlic, minced

¼ tsp salt

Pinch of pepper

### TOPPING

3 zucchini, very thinly sliced

2 bunches asparagus spears, grilled or steamed

6 tbsps basil pesto

Fresh basil leaves and micro greens, to garnish

Preheat the oven to 220°C (425°F, Gas Mark 7). Line a baking tray with baking paper and brush with oil.

Place half the cauliflower in a food processor and pulse until finely chopped and appearing like rice. Transfer to a bowl and repeat with the remaining half.

Cover the bowl with plastic wrap and microwave on high for 5 minutes until softened. Tip onto a clean tea towel and allow to cool slightly. Squeeze as much liquid as you can out of the cauliflower by wringing the tea towel over the sink. Transfer to a clean bowl. Add the almond meal, eggs, mixed herbs and salt and pepper and mix well to combine.

Scoop the cauliflower mix into the centre of the tray, then press out into a round. Create a slightly thicker crust at the edges. Transfer to the oven and bake for 15 minutes or until golden brown at the edges.

Place the ingredients for the tomato sauce in a bowl and stir to combine.

Smear tomato paste on the entire base, then add zucchini slices to cover. Place asparagus spears on top and then drizzle the pesto over. Return to the oven for another 5 minutes to heat through.

Remove from the oven and serve, garnished with fresh basil and micro greens.

# Takeaway Fish and Chips

MAKE THEM AT HOME, WRAP UP IN PAPER, AND EAT IN THE PARK
OR THE GARDEN FOR EXTRA FRIDAY NIGHT FUN WITH THE KIDS

**SERVES 4**

4 snapper, skinned
and deboned

1 egg, beaten

Salt and pepper, to
season

1 cup (125g, 4oz)
whole wheat panko
breadcrumbs

1 tbsp olive oil

1kg (2lb) potatoes,
peeled and sliced into
chips

Vegetable oil, to
deep-fry

Tartare sauce, lemon
wedges, sea salt flakes,
to serve

Preheat the oven to 245°C (475°F, Gas Mark 9). Line a rimmed
baking tray with aluminum foil and lightly oil. Set aside.

Cut the fish into 8 pieces.

Place the egg in a large bowl and season with salt and pepper. In
another bowl combine the panko and olive oil. Dip the fish into
the egg (shaking off any excess) and then into the panko. Press
the panko crumbs onto the fish to be sure that they stick and
then place each breaded piece of fish onto the prepared tray.

Transfer to the oven to cook for 15 minutes or until crunchy on
the outside and fish is cooked through.

Pat potatoes dry to remove excess moisture. Heat oil over a high
heat in a large saucepan or deep-frying pan. Deep-fry chips in
batches until lightly golden. Transfer to a tray lined with paper
towel to absorb excess oil. Repeat until all chips are fried.

Arrange fish on top of chips and serve with tartare sauce, lemon
wedges and salt to taste.

**NOTE:** If you can't find snapper, substitute any firm white-
fleshed fish. You can use regular breadcrumbs instead of panko.
Panko is recommended here for the extra crunch factor it
provides.

# THEME NIGHTS!

An excellent way to try out new, heathy foods that might seem strange to children (and adults who are a tad stuck in their ways) is to serve them up with a story. Also, why not bring the world to the dinner table — it's a way to travel if there's not quite the budget for a round-the-globe ticket for a family of four.

Pick a night of the week to visit Singapore, Italy, or what about Jamaica? Try to get familiar with a country's classic dishes and experiment too. How about a chicken burger with Asian coriander served in a soft taco shell? Or add a mild curry sauce to the average toasted cheese sandwich. The family might start writing its own cookbook.

## AROUND THE WORLD AT DINNERTIME

MEXICAN: It's one of the most popular cuisines in the world as much for its fresh and vibrant flavours as for the fun value — the kids can wear sombreros and maybe an adult can take out a guitar while the family gorge on healthy taco fillings like chicken or fish and fresh coleslaw. For starters, experiment with varieties of guacamole — get tropical with pineapple or mango, or add Parmesan and basil and visit Rome and Mexico City in one night. Entice the kids with a big bowl of taco chips with guacamole and gooey cheese.

THAI: Rice noodles with peanut sauce are a simple, scrumptious version of the pad thai that's so beloved in Thai restaurants. Blend peanut butter with lime juice, soy sauce, garlic and a dash of brown sugar. Pour it over the noodles and eat just like that or add healthy toppings like barbecued chicken tenders — which can be put on skewers for a Thai starter — and Chinese broccoli. The peanut sauce can keep in the fridge or the freezer for another Asian feast — add it to potatoes and sprinkle on some chilli for a take on a potato curry. Cut up lime into quarters and squeeze on top for as much zest as desired.

JAPANESE: Making sushi rolls at home is not difficult, though it does take a bit of learning. Most international food aisles stock the sushi rice, the seaweed and the sauces. Sushi-grade salmon or tuna are good for starter taste buds or better yet, start with wrapping raw vegetables like carrot, celery and cucumber into rice, then maybe a tin of tuna for protein. Baby steps. Parents and kids can learn together. However, there's no need to get fancy — try Japanese soba noodles with sesame seeds and a light soy sauce marinade, tossed through with crunchy vegetables. Or lay smoked salmon and pickled ginger over a bowl of rice. After the first time, these theme nights are a breeze.

# Mexican Enchilada

A DISH FOR KEEPS, THESE ENCHILADAS WILL BECOME A FIRM
FAMILY FAVOURITE AFTER THE FIRST MOUTHFUL

**SERVES 4-6**

1 tbsp olive oil

2 cloves garlic, crushed

2 cups (450g, 16oz) tomato salsa

2 large chicken breasts

2 cups (250g, 8oz) tasty cheese, shredded, divided (use pre-grated pizza cheese mix if you like!)

¼ cup (60ml, 2fl oz) sour cream

55g (2oz) cream cheese

½ cup (20g, ¾ oz) plus 1 tbsp fresh coriander, roughly chopped, divided

1 tsp ground cumin

12 flour tortillas

¾ cup (185ml, 6fl oz) sour cream, to serve

In a large, deep frying pan heat the olive oil and fry the crushed garlic for 1 minute. Add the salsa to the garlic and heat until it starts to boil.

Place the chicken breast in the pan, bring down the heat to low and cover the chicken. Let it cook for 15 minutes. Turn off the heat, remove the chicken from the sauce and let both cool.

Preheat the oven to 220°C (430°F, Gas Mark 7).

Using two forks, shred the chicken breasts by holding the chicken steady with one fork and using the other to scrape and tear away shreds of chicken. Transfer the shredded chicken to a large bowl. Add ½ cup of the sauce, 1½ cups cheese, the sour cream, cream cheese, ½ cup coriander, and the cumin. Mix thoroughly.

Spoon the chicken mixture along the centre of each tortilla. The mixture should be divided equally between the tortillas.

In a 28 x 18cm (11 x 7in) deep-sided baking dish, spread ½ cup of the sauce mix.

Roll up the tortillas and place seam-side down in the dish, sitting them snugly next to each other. Spread over the remaining sauce and then sprinkle over the rest of the cheese, followed by the tablespoon of coriander.

Bake the enchiladas in the oven, uncovered, for 8-10 minutes or until the tortillas are just beginning to turn golden.

Reduce the oven temperature to 200°C (390°F, Gas Mark 6). Lightly cover the dish with aluminum foil and bake for 20 minutes. Carefully remove the foil after 20 minutes and bake, uncovered, for an additional 5 minutes or until the cheese is golden.

The enchiladas will be very hot once you take them out of the oven, so let them cool down for at least 10 minutes before serving. Serve with a dollop of sour cream.

# Fish Tacos with Mango Salsa

FINGER - LICKING GOOD TACOS THAT ARE FULL OF FLAVOUR AND GREAT FUN TO EAT AS A FAMILY MEAL

**SERVES 4**

### MANGO SALSA

1 mango, chopped

1 cucumber, finely chopped

½ red onion, finely chopped

Handful of coriander leaves

1 tbsp lime juice

Salt and pepper, to taste

### FISH

⅓ cup (40g, 1½ oz) plain flour

½ tsp salt

¼ tsp freshly ground pepper

¼ tsp smoked paprika

3-4 snapper fillets

2 tbsps vegetable oil

### TO SERVE

12 tortillas

¼ head small red cabbage, shredded

Sour cream, to taste

1 avocado, sliced

¼ bunch coriander, leaves picked

To make the mango salsa, simply combine the ingredients together in a small bowl. Cover and place in the fridge until ready to use.

To prepare the fish, place the flour, salt, pepper and paprika in a shallow container or on a plate and mix together.

Check the fish for bones and scales. Rinse and pat the fish dry, then dredge it in the flour mixture.

Heat the oil in a heavy-based frying pan over a medium-high heat until shimmering. Place fish fillets side by side in the pan. Cook for 3 minutes, then carefully flip and cook for 2 minutes on the other side until fish is opaque and flakes apart easily at the thickest part of the fillet. Remove from the heat. Gently cut the fish into slices and place on a plate. Cover with aluminium foil to keep warm.

Quickly heat each tortilla for 10-15 seconds on the grill.

To serve, divide red cabbage, mango salsa, sour cream, avocado and coriander between the tortillas and top with the fish.

# Chilli con Carne with Cheese

A ONE-POT WONDER THAT'S THE PERFECT WARMER ON A COLD WINTER'S NIGHT — GREAT WITH RICE OR BAKED POTATOES

**SERVES 6**

1 tbsp olive oil

1 onion, chopped

1 capsicum, finely chopped

1 red chilli, finely chopped

2 cloves garlic, minced

2 tsps dried oregano

2 tsps ground cumin

1 tsp ground cinnamon

1 tsp smoked paprika

½ tsp chilli flakes (adjust to taste)

1 tsp ground coriander

500g (1lb 2oz) beef mince

1 x 400g (14oz) can diced tomatoes

½ cup (125ml, 4fl oz) water

1 x 400g (14oz) kidney beans, drained and rinsed

Cheddar cheese, to serve

Heat the oil in a large saucepan over a medium-high heat. Add the onion, capsicum, chilli and garlic and fry for 4 minutes.

Add the oregano, cumin, cinnamon, paprika, chilli flakes and coriander and stir to combine. Cook for 1-2 minutes to let the flavours infuse.

Increase the heat to high. Add mince and brown, stirring constantly, for 7-8 minutes.

Add the tomatoes and water. Reduce the heat to a simmer and cook for 10 minutes.

Add kidney beans and simmer for 10 minutes, until sauce thickens.

Serve sprinkled with a generous amount of grated Cheddar cheese.

# Black Bean, Corn and Quinoa Salad

THIS COLOURFUL AND HEALTHY SALAD MAKES THE PERFECT ADDITION TO YOUR WEEKNIGHT DINNER MENU

**SERVES 8**

1 cup (250ml, 8fl oz) vegetable stock

½ cup (100g, 3oz) quinoa (well rinsed)

½ tbsp olive oil

¼ tsp ground cumin

¼ tsp ground oregano

¼ tsp cayenne pepper

1 cup (170g, 6oz) fresh corn kernels

1 x 400g (14oz) can black beans (rinsed and drained)

½ red onion, finely chopped

¾ cup (150g, 5oz) Roma tomatoes, chopped

3 tsps fresh lime juice

1 avocado, diced

Salt and pepper, to taste

1 tbsp fresh parsley, chopped

2 limes, cut into wedges

In a saucepan, bring stock to a boil. Add quinoa, cover, and simmer on low heat until water is absorbed, 10-15 minutes. Cool.

In a small frying pan, heat the olive oil on medium heat. Add the cumin, oregano and cayenne and fry for about 30 seconds. Add the corn kernels and cook over high heat for 3 minutes, stirring constantly until the kernels begin to char slightly on the outside. Reduce the heat back to medium and add the black beans, stirring gently to heat them through for 2 minutes.

In a large bowl, combine the quinoa, onion, tomato and lime juice.

Stir in the corn and bean mix. Then gently mix in the avocado, trying to keep the cubes whole.

Season with salt and pepper, sprinkle over the parsley and serve warm with the lime wedges.

# Sweet & Sour Prawns

# Coconut Rice

**SERVES 4**

¾ cup (120g, 4oz) brown sugar

1 tbsp cornflour

1 x 225g (8oz) can pineapple pieces with juice

⅓ cup (80ml, 3fl oz) vinegar

⅓ cup (80ml, 3fl oz) water

1 tbsp soy sauce

Olive oil, for frying

500g (1lb 2oz, around 20) large green prawns, peeled and deveined, tails intact

Combine the brown sugar, cornflour, pineapple, vinegar, water and soy sauce in a medium-sized saucepan over a medium-high heat.

Bring to a boil, stirring constantly. Reduce heat to a simmer and cover. Simmer for 5 minutes, stirring occasionally until desired thickness is reached.

Heat oil in a large frying pan. When very hot add prawns and cook for 2 minutes, stirring occasionally until opaque and cooked through. Pour sauce over the prawns and gently toss to coat.

**SERVES 4**

1¼ cups (310ml, 10fl oz) chicken stock

1 cup (250ml, 8fl oz) coconut milk

½ tsp salt

1 cup (155g, 4oz) basmati rice

Spring onion and black sesame seeds, to garnish

Combine the stock, coconut milk and salt in a large saucepan over a medium-high heat. Bring to a boil, then reduce the heat to a gentle simmer.

Add the rice and stir constantly for 1 minute.

Cover the pan and simmer over low heat, undisturbed, for 15 minutes.

Remove from the heat and set aside for 10 minutes.

Remove lid, fluff rice with a fork and garnish before serving.

# PRAWNS

Starting early in life with prawns may be a path to a healthy appetite and perhaps a turn on some celebrity chef show later in life! Barbecued prawns are such delicious finger food — salty, buttery, chewy. How perfect to hand a child an entire creature to marvel at, then devour while getting a significant dose of the day's iron requirements, along with zinc for healing and vitamin E for soft, bare-arm cuddles. Seafood is the stuff of lasting childhood memories. For a full meal, chop up and toss into whole wheat spaghetti.

# Carrot Risotto

A DREAMY, CREAMY WAY OF GETTING VITAMIN A INTO YOUR KIDS — THEY'LL LOVE THIS EASY-TO-EAT RISOTTO

**SERVES 6**

1 tbsp olive oil

1 tbsp butter

6 carrots, grated

6 cups (1.5L, 50fl oz) vegetable stock

55g (2oz) butter

2 medium (300g, 10oz) onions, chopped

2 cloves garlic, finely chopped

2 cups (310g, 8oz) Arborio rice

½ cup (125ml) dry white wine

60g (2oz) marscapone

½ cup (60g, 2oz) Parmesan cheese, grated, 2 tbsps reserved for garnish

Salt and pepper, to taste

Preheat the oven to 200°C (400°F, Gas Mark 6) and line a baking tray with greaseproof paper.

Heat the oil and butter over medium heat in a frying pan. Add carrots and stir with a wooden spoon until well coated. Cook, stirring, for 5 minutes until soft. Remove half of the carrots and set aside. Transfer the remaining carrots to a blender and process until a puree forms.

Meanwhile, bring stock to a gentle simmer in a medium saucepan. Reduce heat to very low and cover pan.

Melt butter in a large saucepan over a medium high heat. Add onion and cook, stirring, for 3-4 minutes until soft. Add garlic and rice and cook, stirring to coat well, for 1 minute. Pour in wine and simmer, uncovered, until liquid has reduced.

Reduce heat to low and add stock to the rice ½ cup at a time until the liquid has fully absorbed. Stir constantly. Stir in carrot puree half way through the process. The risotto is done when the rice is tender but still firm to bite and the risotto is creamy. Add more stock, if required, to achieve this consistency and cook for a further 5 minutes.

Remove risotto from heat. Stir in the marscapone and Parmesan cheese. Season. Serve topped with reserved Parmesan cheese.

# RICE

Rice in all its variations is eaten for breakfast, lunch and dinner in half of the world. It's affordable and nutritious and can transform one meal into three. And it's so easy to eat for tender tooth-growing mouths and fussy tastebuds.

## COOK IT REAL GOOD

The best way to cook rice is a hot topic. Here's the lowdown:

- Buy a rice cooker! It's easy, efficient and gets the job done.
- Whatever method you use, rinse the rice first. This removes any debris along with the starchy surface that can cause rice to be clumpy.
- Use the absorbtion method: cooking on a stove top in a ratio of 1 cup water to 1 cup rice. The rice is cooked and then steamed in the pot. (Note older rice may require more water to cook, which is a tricky variable to manage.)
- Boil it like pasta: just cover the rice with plenty of water (no need to measure) and let it boil away until tender. Drain and serve.

## STARTER GUIDE TO RICES

BROWN RICE: Brown rice is white rice with the hull still attached. The hull is packed with fibre, vitamins and minerals that keep hearts healthy and muscles growing. Brown rice is nuttier and less sweet than white rice. Don't be shy with sauces and flavours — try adding almond milk and maple syrup for a rice pudding.

BASMATI RICE: Common in Asian and Mediterranean restaurants, basmati is known to be 'fragrant', which means that it has a gentle floral flavour. It comes to life with seasonings like lemon, cumin and coriander.

LONG-GRAIN RICE: Perhaps not surprisingly, these rice kernels are long and slim. Boiled and steamed, they are dry and firm and soak up the sauce of a curry or lighter, more summery dressings like olive oil, lemon, salt and pepper. (Throw on an avocado and … yum.)

QUICK-COOK RICE: For the busy parent, this is a perfectly fine choice — it has been half cooked and is ready for a quick steam or microwave. It has slightly fewer nutrients, which can be taken care of with a topping of vegetables and fish (or fish fingers!).

BLACK RICE: This is a less processed rice with flat, wide brownish-black grains. It becomes tender when soaked and then steamed. It is served in Asia and Asian restaurants as a sweet and crunchy dessert with coconut milk and palm sugar.

# Mushroom Risotto

A GREAT GO-TO RECIPE THAT'S EASY TO LEARN BY HEART; ADD SOME CHOPS ON THE SIDE IF YOUR FAMILY ARE 'MUST HAVE MEAT' TYPES

**SERVES 6**

5 cups (1.25L, 42fl oz) chicken stock (or vegetable stock)

3 tbsps butter

1 onion, finely chopped

400g (14oz) Swiss brown mushrooms, thickly sliced

1 tbsp thyme leaves (or dried thyme)

2 cups (310g, 8oz) Arborio rice

½ cup (125ml) dry white wine

½ cup (60g, 2oz) Parmesan cheese, grated

Salt and black pepper, to season

Parmesan shavings, to serve

Fresh thyme, to serve

Bring the stock to a gentle simmer in a medium saucepan. Reduce heat to very low and cover pan.

Melt the butter in a deep-sided medium-sized saucepan over medium-high heat. Add onion and cook, stirring, for 3-4 minutes until soft. Add mushrooms and thyme and saute for 5 minutes. Add the rice and stir to combine.

Pour in the wine and simmer, uncovered, for a minute or two until the liquid has reduced. Reduce heat to low and add stock to the rice ½ cup at a time until the liquid has fully absorbed. Stir constantly. The risotto is done when the rice is tender but still firm to bite and the risotto is creamy.

Stir in the Parmesan cheese and season to taste with salt and pepper. Garnish with shaved Parmesan and fresh thyme.

# Baked Fish in Crunchy Breadcrumbs

AN EASY WEEKNIGHT SUPPER THAT APPEALS TO ADULTS AND KIDS ALIKE — SERVE WITH FROZEN PEAS TO KEEP IT SUPER EASY

**SERVES 4**

¾ cup (90g, 3oz) Parmesan cheese, finely grated

¾ cup (90g, 3oz) panko breadcrumbs (or use standard breadcrumbs)

3 tbsps butter, softened

3 tbsps mayonnaise

1 tsp Worcestershire sauce

½ tsp Tabasco or other hot pepper sauce

2 tbsps flat-leaf parsley leaves, chopped

½ lemon, juiced

4 white fish fillets

Salt and pepper, to season

Few parsley leaves, to garnish

Preheat the oven to 220°C (425°F, Gas Mark 7) and butter a shallow baking dish.

Mix together the cheese, breadcrumbs, butter, mayonnaise, Worcestershire sauce, Tabasco, parsley and lemon juice in a medium-sized bowl. Set aside.

Pat the fish fillets dry with paper towels and season with salt and pepper. Place fish into the baking dish and spread the cheese mixture over each fillet.

Transfer to the oven and bake for 10 minutes, until fish is cooked through and flakes easily with a fork, and the breadcrumbs are golden and crunchy.

Remove from the oven, garnish with fresh parsley and serve immediately.

# Ravioli with Green Peas and Pesto

LEARN HOW TO MAKE YOUR OWN RAVIOLI, OR BUY IT READY-MADE AND
MAKE THIS FRESH PASTA DINNER IN LESS THAN 20 MINUTES

**SERVES 4**

## PASTA DOUGH

1 tsp olive oil

1 tsp salt

¼ cup (60ml, 2fl oz) warm water

4 cups (500g, 1lb) plain flour

200g (7oz) fine semolina

6 eggs

## FILLING

1 tbsp olive oil

2 bunches spinach, leaves picked, steamed and chopped

800g (1¾ lb) firm ricotta

1½ cups (190g, 6oz) grated Parmesan cheese

2 egg yolks

½ tsp ground nutmeg

## OR

500g (1lb 2oz) pkt store-bought fresh ravioli with spinach and ricotta filling

## SAUCE

1 x 190g (7oz) jar pre-made pesto sauce

1 cup (170g, 6oz) frozen peas

## TO SERVE

Fresh herbs, Parmesan cheese and black pepper

**TO MAKE YOUR OWN PASTA DOUGH:** Mix the olive oil, salt and warm water in a small bowl. Sift flour and semolina in a large bowl and create a well in the middle. Crack the eggs into the centre of the well, then add oil mixture. Gradually mix the wet ingredients with the flour using fingers until a dough comes together. Knead the dough on a clean work surface for 10-15 minutes or until smooth. Shape into a ball, cover in plastic wrap and set aside to rest for 30 minutes.

**TO MAKE YOUR OWN FILLING:** Place filling ingredients in a bowl and stir to combine. Cover and refrigerate until ready to use.

Divide the pasta dough into 4 portions. One piece at a time, flatten the dough on a lightly floured work surface. Pass the dough several times through the widest setting on a pasta machine, folding it in half each time. Once smooth, reduce the settings one notch at time until the second-last setting. Lay the pasta on a floured surface. Place 1 teaspoon of filling at intervals along the bottom half of the pasta. Fold the top half over, then press the sides to seal well. Cut the pasta into bite-sized pieces and place on a tray dusted with semolina. Cover and refrigerate until ready to cook.

Place the pesto sauce in a large saucepan over a medium-low heat and gently warm it.

Bring a large saucepan of salted water and a small saucepan of water to the boil. Drop the ravioli (home-made or store bought) into the large pan and simmer for 5 minutes or until al dente. Drain. Drop the peas into the small saucepan and simmer for 3-4 minutes, then drain. Transfer the ravioli and to the saucepan containing the pesto and gently toss to coat. Use a little of the pasta water to create a more liquid consistency if desired.

Serve scattered with herbs, cheese and black pepper.

# THYME

Thyme, such a delicious little herb — but fiddly.
Conventional wisdom is to hold one end firmly in your
fingertips and pull down on the leaves so that they come
off — with varying degress of success perhaps. So try this:
poke the base of the stem through a fine mesh strainer and
pull down so that the stem moves through the strainer
and the leaves collect within. So easy!

# Home-Made Gravy

**SERVES 4**

3 tsps butter

1 garlic clove, finely chopped

3 tbsps plain flour

2 cups (500ml, 1pt) chicken broth or stock

Salt and pepper, to taste

Place the butter in a saucepan over a medium heat and cook until melted. Stir in the garlic and cook for 1 minute.

Slowly whisk in the flour to avoid lumps. 'Cook out' the flour for 2-3 minutes over a medium-low heat, then add the chicken broth or stock slowly, whisking vigorously.

Cook for a further 2-5 minutes, depending on your preferred consistency. Cooking for longer will thicken the gravy. Add more broth or stock for a thinner gravy.

Season to taste with salt and pepper.

# Roast Chicken with Pan Gravy

**SERVES 4**

2 tsps butter

1 chicken, weighing 1.5 kg (3lb 5oz)

Salt and pepper, to taste

1 tbsp plain flour

1 cup (250ml, 8fl oz) chicken stock

Preheat the oven to 200°C (400°F, Gas Mark 6).

Rub butter into the the breast and legs of the chicken, then season the skin with salt and pepper. Place in a roasting pan and transfer to the oven and cook, undisturbed, for 1 hour 20 minutes. To check if chicken is done, pierce the thigh with a skewer and the juices should run clear.

Remove from the oven and, using a pair of tongs, lift the chicken and place into a low-sided dish (to catch the juices). Cover with aluminium foil to keep warm. Allow to rest for 15 minutes.

**TO MAKE THE PAN GRAVY:** Place the roasting pan with its juices over a low heat. Add the flour and stir until a sandy paste forms. Gradually pour in the stock, stirring constantly, until thickened. Simmer for 2 minutes, stirring. Pour in any extra juices from the chicken dish and then serve.

# Sticky Chicken Drumsticks

THIS POPULAR EAT-WITH-YOUR FINGERS FOOD IS A HIT WITH MOST KIDS AND ONLY NEEDS A SIMPLE SALAD AND RICE TO GO WITH IT

**SERVES 4**

8 chicken drumsticks

**MARINADE**

¼ cup (90g, 3oz) maple syrup

3 tbsps olive oil

1 clove garlic, crushed

1 tbsp fresh ginger, finely grated

¼ tsp turmeric powder

1 tbsp paprika

Freshly ground black pepper, to garnish

Rinse the drumsticks under cool water and pat dry with paper towel.

Combine the marinade ingredients in a small bowl.

Coat the drumsticks with the marinade. Cover with foil and let sit for at least 1 hour in the fridge.

Preheat the oven to 240°C (465°F, Gas Mark 9).

Line a baking dish with foil and lay out the drumsticks on the foil.

Bake the drumsticks in the oven for 30 minutes, turning halfway through.

The skin should be browned and slightly sticky and crispy and the chicken must be cooked all the way through.

Garnish with black pepper.

# Honey Roast Vegetables and Crispy Potatoes

## FULL OF FLAVOUR, THIS IS A WONDERFUL AND EASY ACCOMPANIMENT TO THE SUNDAY ROAST OR WEEKDAY CHOPS OR STEAK

**SERVES 4**

3 tbsps olive oil, divided

1 bunch of Dutch carrots, scrubbed

4 medium potatoes, peeled and cut into chunks

1 large red onion, cut into chunks

Salt and freshly ground black pepper

1 tbsp rosemary, chopped (plus more sprigs to garnish)

2 tbsps honey

Preheat the oven to 200°C (400°F, Gas Mark 6).

Toss the cut vegetables with olive oil.

Brush a roasting pan with oil and place in the oven for 5 minutes so to heat up the oil.

Put the carrots, potatoes and onion in the roasting pan and add the rest of the olive oil, tossing to coat. Transfer to the oven and roast for 20 minutes. Sprinkle with salt and pepper and add the chopped rosemary. Stir a couple of times to rotate the vegetables.

Return to the oven and bake on a high shelf for 30 minutes, turning occasionally to ensure even browning.

Spoon the honey into the roasting pan and toss together so that the vegetables are coated. Roast for a further 5-10 minutes until glazed and golden.

Serve garnished with rosemary sprigs.

# Freezer Friendly

# SOUPS

Is there any better comforter after cold mornings on the soccer field — or in teary moments — than a bowl of warm soup? And how else to feed an army of family and friends than a couple of hot pots on the party table? Soups are also a crafty way to disguise foods that might otherwise feel like punishment to small beings — add some salty liquid, a little cream and maybe bacon to a mound of broccoli and it will go down like a dream.

Generally, making soup is about taking ingredients from the crisper, throwing them in a big pan, adding water and a few spices and leaving it to simmer, simmer, simmer. Then there are a couple of tricks for making home-made soup irresistible.

## A PRESENT FOR THE SOUP CUPBOARD

A blender or a food processor is not essential but helps many a soup chef get creative with textures. You can go for the classic bowl blender. Or treat the family kitchen to a hand-held stick or immersion blender and puree right in the saucepan. This avoids transferring from the hot pan to the cool blender bowl. Also, little hands can join in the process — nothing like standing on a stool next to the stove from a young age to plant the seed for the next home chef! A blender can take a chunky soup to a divine puree in a few minutes — and it's fun to watch happen.

## HOME-MADE STOCKS

It might seem complicated, yet it just takes one good home-brewed stock to convert. And the advantage is it can be frozen and used for months.

CHICKEN STOCK: Throw the carcass of the family roast chicken — and maybe some extra wings — in with leeks, onions, celery, carrots, bay leaves, parsley, salt, pepper and water. Bring to a boil, simmer for around 4 hours, then cool in the fridge. Voila.

VEGETABLE STOCK: Do the same as above, minus the chicken, and simmer for about 2 hours. Extra celery, maybe. Super easy and fresh.

## GARNISHES — THE FUN IS IN THE DETAILS

- The Dollop: for creaminess, add a spoon of sour cream, yoghurt or creme fraiche.
- The Crush: take a rolling pin to a bag of croutons, sesame or pumpkin seeds and add crunch to a creamy puree.
- The Crumble: add cream and zest with a sprinkling of feta, ricotta or goat's cheese. Or get salty and grainy with grated Parmesan or pecorino.
- The Spice: try chilli flakes for zing (that the kids can just avoid with the spoon).

# Minestrone Soup

THIS IS ONE OF THOSE SOUPS THAT'S REALLY A MEAL — SERVE WITH
PLENTY OF TOAST AND BUTTER AND THAT'S DINNER DONE

**SERVES 4**

2 tbsps olive oil

1 onion, chopped

4 carrots, diced

4 celery stalks, chopped

2 cloves garlic, peeled

1 x 400g (14oz) can chopped tomatoes

3½ cups (875ml, 30fl oz) vegetable stock

150g (5oz) spaghetti, broken into pieces

Parmesan cheese rind (optional)

1 x 400g (14oz) can kidney beans

Handful of spinach (fresh or frozen), chopped

1 cup (170g, 6oz) frozen peas

Salt and pepper

Grated Parmesan cheese and fresh parsley leaves, to serve

In a large saucepan, heat the olive oil over medium heat.

Add the onion, carrots and celery and saute until the vegetables are softened.

Grate in the garlic and cook for another 2 minutes, stirring so the garlic doesn't burn.

Add the chopped tomatoes, stock, spaghetti and Parmesan rind (if using), bring to a simmer and cook for 7-8 minutes until the spaghetti is almost cooked. Add the beans, spinach and peas and cook for a further 2-3 minutes.

Season to taste with salt and pepper and and serve hot with freshly grated Parmesan cheese and fresh parsley.

**NOTE:** Don't forget to use leftover spaghetti or tinned tomatoes for this recipe if you have them in the fridge.

# Mushroom Soup

THIS CREAMY, RUSTIC-STYLE SOUP MAKES FOR A LOVELY LIGHT DINNER — OUT OF THE FREEZER AND ONTO THE TABLE IN MINUTES

**SERVES 4**

1 tbsp olive oil

1 small onion, chopped

2¼ cups (200g, 7oz) button mushrooms, sliced

2 potatoes, peeled and diced

3 cups (750ml, 24fl oz) vegetable stock

2 cups (500ml, 1pt) water

Black pepper, to garnish

Crusty bread, to serve

Heat oil in a large saucepan over medium heat. Add onion and fry, stirring occasionally, for 4 minutes, or until it starts to soften. Add the mushrooms (retaining some to garnish the soup) and fry for a further 4-5 minutes until tender.

Add potatoes, stock and water to the saucepan and bring to the boil. Reduce heat to medium-low and simmer, covered, for 20 minutes, or until potatoes are very tender.

Remove from the heat. Set aside to cool slightly. Remove two spoonfuls of the potatoes with a slotted spoon and set aside for a moment. Transfer the rest of the soup to a blender and process in batches, or use an immersion blender in the pot, until smooth.

Return soup and retained potatoes to the saucepan. Heat over medium heat until hot. Season with salt and pepper.

Ladle soup into bowls. Top with retained mushrooms and fresh black pepper. Serve with crusty bread.

# Red Lentil Soup

A HEALTHY OPTION THANKS TO SOME SNEAKY VEGETABLES AND THE NUTRIENT - AND - FIBRE - RICH STARRING INGREDIENT, LENTILS

**SERVES 4**

1 tbsp olive oil

1 onion, diced

1 carrot, diced

2 stalks celery, diced

½ red capsicum, diced

¼ tsp salt

1 cup (185g, 6oz) red lentils

4 cups (1L, 2pt) vegetable stock (or water)

1 bay leaf

2 tbsps lemon juice

Salt and freshly ground pepper, to taste

Heat the oil in a large saucepan over a medium heat.

Add the onion, carrot, celery, capsicum and salt and stir to combine. Reduce the heat to low. Cover with a lid and sweat the vegetables for 5 minutes, until onion is soft and translucent.

Add the lentils, stock and bay leaf.

Increase the heat and bring to the boil. Lower the heat and simmer for 20 minutes, until lentils are soft and breaking apart.

Remove from the heat and stir in the lemon juice.

Discard the bay leaf and season with salt and fresh pepper, to taste, before serving.

# Chicken Pasta Soup

**SERVES 4**

1 onion, finely chopped

2 chicken breast fillets, cut into small pieces

2 tbsps olive oil

1 carrot, sliced

6 cups (1.5L, 50fl oz) chicken stock

100g (3½ oz) pasta spirals

2 tbsps flat-leaf parsley leaves, chopped

Salt and pepper, to taste

Fry onions and chicken in oil in a saucepan over medium heat for 5 minutes, until onions are softened and chicken lightly browned. Add carrot and cook for 2 further minutes.

Add stock and cover saucepan. Bring to the boil, then reduce heat and allow to simmer for 15 minutes.

Add pasta and simmer for a further 10 minutes, until pasta is soft.

When soup is ready to serve, mix in parsley and season with salt and pepper.

# Carrot Soup

**SERVES 4**

2 tbsps olive oil

1 onion, chopped

6 carrots, diced

3 cups (750ml, 24fl oz) vegetable stock

¼ tsp chilli flakes (optional)

Salt and pepper, to taste

Sour cream and herbs, to garnish

Heat olive oil in a large saucepan over medium-high heat. Add onion and fry, stirring, for 5 minutes, or until translucent. Then add carrots and cook for 1-2 minutes, stirring.

Add stock and bring to a boil. Reduce heat to low, then add chilli flakes (if using) and season with salt and pepper. Cook on a gentle simmer for 20 minutes until carrots are very tender.

Turn off heat and allow soup to cool slightly. Add to the blender in batches and puree until smooth, or use an immersion blender in the pot.

Return to the pot and stir. Add water for a thinner consistency. Serve warm with crusty bread, garnished with chopped herbs and sour cream.

# MAKE YOUR OWN PASTRY

Puff pastry, French pastry, sweet pastry, Danish pastry, pastry for pie crust, filo pastry: so many pastries to spend a bunch of Saturday afternoons learning and experimenting with. For the most part, all are a combination of flour, water, milk and eggs — and how they end up on the dinner table is in the details, including the time and muscle strength that goes into turning the gooey dough into the final crumbly, crunchy, flaky or dense and always melt-in-the-mouth product.

## PASTRY PARTY

All that's really needed for a pastry party is adventurous little fingers and the imagination that come from young minds. For inspiration, there are also pastry making kits that come with cutters in the shape of hearts and triangles and flowers and trees.

Invite the friends over to a workshop afternoon followed by a buttery, flaky, delicious feast.

CHEESY STAR PUFF PASTRIES: The star shape is a favourite for Christmas time but it doesn't need to wait. Add the little ones' favourite cheese to the dough or sprinkle it on top for an exciting snack that's just as healthy as a cheese sandwich.

DANISH CLASSICS: The envelope, the pinwheel and the pocket are traditional shapes for Danish pastries, which are bite-sized, chewy puff pastry cases filled with a sweet cheese and fruit spread.

PET PASTRIES: Why not turn snack time into a visit to the backyard jungle. Have the children practise drawing on paper the shapes of dogs, dinosaurs, horses, rabbits or cats — just a head with ears and whiskers will do — then transfer that drawing to the pastry and cut around it with a sharp butter knife. Once baked, decorate with icing. A rainbow-striped dog makes the real world all that more colourful.

NUTELLA TURNOVERS: A turnover is a triangle filled with goodness and what can be better than a nutty, chocolate spread that oozes out when the kids bite into it. Turnovers can be made into lots of different shapes. Try love hearts, half moons or simple flower shapes with just a few big petals. Close the edges with a butter knife and a fork.

## TIP

- Moisturize the pastry with a beaten egg, using a soft food brush so that the pastry doesn't dry while the shapes are forming.
- Include paper and pen in the workshop and encourage drawing the shapes before letting loose on the pastry.

# Country-Style Chicken Pie

TAKE THE PRE-MADE FILLING AND PASTRIES OUT OF THE FREEZER AND THIS HEARTY CHICKEN PIE IS AN EASY CHOICE FOR DINNER

**SERVES 4**

2 tbsps olive oil

6 chicken thigh fillets, cut into pieces

1 onion, chopped

1 carrot, peeled, sliced

1 stalk celery, sliced

2 tbsps plain flour

1 cup (250ml, 8fl oz) chicken stock

½ cup (70g, 2½ oz) frozen corn kernels

¼ cup (60ml, 2fl oz) cream

Salt and pepper. to taste

1 sheet ready-made shortcrust pastry

1 sheet ready-made puff pastry

1 egg, beaten

Place 1 tablespoon of oil in a frying pan over a high heat. Add the chicken in batches (according to the size of the pan) and fry, stirring often, until meat is nicely browned all over. Transfer the chicken to a bowl and set aside.

Place the other tablespoon of oil in the same pan over a medium heat, and add the onion, carrot and celery and cook, stirring, for 5 minutes or until onion softens. Add the flour and stir for 1 minute or until well combined. Add the chicken and stock and bring to the boil. Reduce heat to low and cook, stirring occasionally, for 15 minutes or until chicken is cooked through and sauce thickens. Add the corn and and cream and stir to combine. Remove from heat. Season with salt and pepper.

Preheat oven to 220°C (430°F, Gas Mark 7). Line the base and sides of a pie dish with the shortcrust pastry. Trim the edge. Line with baking paper and fill with a baking weight such as rice or beans. Place in the oven to bake for 10 minutes, then remove the baking weights and discard the paper. Return to the oven to bake for a further 6-8 minutes, or until pastry is just golden.

Scrape the chicken mixture into the pie shell. Drape the puff pastry over the top to enclose the filling and using a small, sharp knife, trim the edge. Lightly brush with egg. Bake in the oven for 15 minutes or until pastry is golden.

# Beef Empanadas

A CRUMBLY, BUTTERY, SPICY TASTE OF MEXICO THAT WILL IMPRESS THE WHOLE FAMILY

**MAKES 24**

### FILLING

1 tbsp olive oil

1 medium onion, finely chopped

2 cloves garlic, crushed

600g (1lb 5oz) beef mince

1 tbsp tomato paste

¼ cup (60ml, 2fl oz) vegetable stock

½ capsicum, finely chopped

3 tbsps paprika

½ tsp cumin

½ tsp cinnamon

½ tsp cayenne

½ tsp salt

¾ cup (90g, 3oz) mozzarella cheese, grated

### PASTRY DOUGH

3¾ cups (465g, 15oz) plain flour

1 tbsp sugar

1½ tsps salt

170g (6oz) butter, straight from the fridge, cut into small cubes

1¼ cups (310ml, 10fl oz) ice water

2 eggs, beaten, for glazing

Heat the olive oil in medium frying pan on medium-high heat. Add the onion and garlic and fry, stirring, for 5 minutes until the onion is golden. Add the mince and cook for 5 minutes until browned. Stir in the tomato paste and stock, then mix through the capsicum, spices and salt. Let sit on a low heat for 10 minutes until the capsicum has softened. Let the mixture cool in the fridge for at least 2 hours. It needs to be quite cool while you're spooning it into the pastry casings.

Next, make the dough. In a food processer, add the flour, sugar and salt. Pulse a few times to combine. Add the butter and pulse again several times until the mixture looks like breadcrumbs. Transfer to a large bowl and add the ice water a bit at a time, mixing it into the dough with a spatula. The dough will form a rough ball — you may not need all the ice water, or you may need slightly more. Split the dough mixture in half and shape each half into a ball. Wrap each in plastic wrap and flatten slightly. Put in the fridge for at least 2 hours.

Preheat oven to 220°C (430°F, Gas Mark 7).

Place the dough on a lightly floured bench. Split each disk into three to help you better roll it out. Roll to a thickness of about 3mm (⅛ in) and cut out circles of around 10cm (4in) diameter. Place these circles onto baking paper on a flat surface.

Take beef mix out of the fridge and stir through the cheese. Place a heaped dessertspoon slightly to the side of the centre of each circle. Wet the pastry around the edge and fold over to form a half-circle. Use a fork to press the edges together, making ridges.

Place on a large baking tray lined with baking paper. Brush lightly with the beaten egg. Bake in the oven for 25 minutes or until golden brown. Once they are cooked, let them sit for at least 5 minutes to cool, then serve.

# Spanakopita (Spinach Pie)

## THE BEST WAY IMAGINABLE TO GET YOUR KIDS EATING SPINACH AND ASKING FOR MORE

**SERVES 6-8**

1 tbsp olive oil

1 medium onion, chopped

300g (10oz) frozen spinach, thawed and drained, chopped

100g (3½ oz) feta cheese

250g (9oz) fresh ricotta cheese (important to use fresh ricotta and not ricotta in a tub)

2 eggs, beaten

½ tsp salt

120g (4oz) unsalted butter (melted)

2 tbsps flat leaf parsley, finely chopped

1 tbsp dill, finely chopped

1 pkt filo pastry

Preheat oven to 190°C (375°F, Gas Mark 5).

In a frying pan, heat the olive oil over medium-high heat. Cook the onion for 6 minutes until softened and golden.

In a large bowl place the onion, spinach, feta, ricotta, egg and salt. Mix until well combined.

Gently place one sheet of filo on a benchtop surface and brush lightly with melted butter (while you're assembling the pie, keep the unused filo covered with a damp tea towel, it needs to be kept moist.)

Place another sheet of filo on top and brush with more butter. Repeat until you have 6 layers but don't brush the top sheet with butter.

Place the layers of filo into a 23 x 4cm (9 x 1½ in) greased pie dish. Pour over this the spinach mixture.

Brush another 6 sheets of filo with butter and place over the spinach mix. Tuck the edges of the pastry down the sides of the dish. Brush the top with any remaining butter.

Bake in the oven for 40 minutes or until the pastry is golden.

Remove and let it sit for 5 minutes to cool before serving.

# DUMPLINGS

Sometimes, it seems the world has gone dumpling crazy, which has been true in large parts of Asia for generations. In China, pieces of dough filled with some sort of meat or vegetable mix are often made into shapes that resemble ancient Chinese money and are said to bring fortune to the household. They are eaten in the New Year and are stuffed with a golden chestnut or a gold coin.

There are so many types of dumplings — in fact, some chefs consider ravioli a dumpling as it fits the description of savoury-filled dough that fits in an adult mouth and takes just a few extra nibbles for more delicate mouths. As their popularity has grown, there are oodles of variations on the traditional. Trendy cafes serve breakfast dumplings filled with bacon and egg. There are 'apple pie' dumplings for dessert. Some fusion restaurants are also getting creative with ingredients and seasonings from different cuisines — pork and cabbage dumplings served with guacamole, for example.

## DUMPLINGS THAT STARTED THE CRAZE

SOUP DUMPLINGS: Served steamed in bamboo baskets, these dumplings are all the rage in Chinatowns across the world. Inside a ball of dough is pork or prawn, soaking in a hot broth that's usually clear and salty. There is an art to eating soup dumplings so the broth inside doesn't scald your mouth — scoop the dumpling onto a deep Chinese spoon, poke it very gently with a chopstick and empty the soup into the spoon. Eat simultaneously for all three textures of dough, broth and meat.

POTSTICKERS: This is another name for a pan-fried dumpling served in Chinese restaurants. (In China, they're called *guo tie*). These are first steamed to preserve their juiciness and then fried to crisp up the bottom layer.

WONTONS: Wontons are smaller and have a thicker dough than potstickers. They look like miniature presents. Wontons are usually filled with prawn or pork and prawn, though chicken, vegetable and crab are also scrumptious. These are the juicy little treasures that are usually floating in a bowl of clear or chicken soup in a Chinese restaurant.

GYOZA: Gyoza are the Japanese version of potstickers. The dough is thinner and sometimes made of rice flour, rather than wheat flour. Minced pork is probably the most popular filling, though vegetarians love gyoza that are filled with a chopped mix of spinach, cabbage and some egg to hold it together. These are served boiled or pan fried, usually with a vinegar dipping sauce.

# Chicken Wontons

**MAKES 40**

450g (1lb) chicken mince

1 tbsp sesame oil

2 tsps fresh ginger, grated

2 small cloves garlic, minced

2 tbsps coriander, finely chopped

1 stalk lemongrass, finely chopped

1 egg, beaten lightly

40 wonton wrappers

Mix together all of the ingredients except wrappers and oil in a large bowl. Set aside. Fill a small bowl with water and line a baking tray with baking paper. Place heaped spoonfuls of the mixture slightly to the side of the centre of each wrapper, moisten the edges with water, fold the edges together to seal. Fold the sides in over the top like a parcel and seal with water. Place each dumpling on the baking paper and repeat until all the filling is used.

To freeze, place uncovered in the freezer for about 2 hours until slightly hard, then place in an airtight container. Remove dumplings from the freezer and cook from frozen in a steamer lined with baking paper over simmering water. Cook in batches for 15 minutes until tender and cooked through.

# Pork Dumplings

**MAKES 40**

450g (1lb) pork mince

¼ cup (25g, 1oz) spring onions, finely chopped

300g (10oz) Chinese cabbage (wombok), finely shredded and chopped

1 tbsp fresh ginger, grated

2 tbsps soy sauce

2 tbsps Chinese rice wine

2 tbsps sesame oil

40 round dumpling wrappers

In a large bowl mix together the pork, spring onions, cabbage, ginger, soy sauce, wine and sesame oil. Fill a small bowl with water and line a baking tray with baking paper. Place heaped spoonfuls of the mixture in the centre of each wrapper, moisten the edges with water, and place in the centre of your palm. Gather up the edges and twist to make a small bag, sealing the edges. Place each completed dumpling on the baking paper and repeat until all the filling is used.

To freeze, see instructions on this page for the chicken wontons.

# BAMBOO STEAMERS

These pretty baskets make light, healthy cooking almost ridiculously easy. Bamboo steamers are the ovens of China — most foods cook in these: vegetables, fish, marinated meat. They're the classic serving dish for dumplings — serve up prawn gyoza still steaming in bamboo. A few tricks to simplify: line the lattice of the steamer with baking paper or giant lettuce leaves to keep the flavours from seeping into the bamboo. Many recipes suggest placing the steamer in a shallow frying pan filled with water. This works but can slowly burn the bamboo. A wok or a large saucepan with sloped sides is better so the steamer sits suspended above the water.

# Prawn Gyoza

SOFT, JUICY AND FRAGRANT, GYOZA ARE THE PERFECT CROWD-PLEASER
AND THE BEST-KEPT SECRET IS: THEY ARE SO EASY TO MAKE

**MAKES 30**

30 wonton wrappers

1 tbsps canola or
vegetable oil for
cooking

**FILLING**

400g (14oz) prawns,
minced

300g (10oz) Chinese
cabbage (wombok),
finely chopped

½ tsp salt

1 tsp cornflour

5 spring onions, finely
chopped

2 tsps fresh ginger,
finely grated

½ tsp soy sauce

1 tbsp mirin

1 tbsp sesame oil

Pinch of white pepper

In a large bowl, mix all the filling ingredients together.

Spoon about a tablespoon of the mixture into the centre of each
dumpling wrapper.

Wet the edge of each wrapper with water and fold the wrappers
over in half while pinching the sides together to close the gyoza.

Heat the oil in a large frying pan over medium heat and place the
gyoza in the pan and let them cook until lightly browned on the
bottom.

Pour ½ cup of water into the pan and put a lid on it to steam the
gyoza for about 5 minutes.

Take the lid off and let the water evaporate.

Turn off the heat and serve.

# YOU CAN'T BEAT FRESH HERBS TO FREEZE

Frozen food has not always had a great reputation — the thinking for many years was that freezing dries out the nutrients and reduces its taste. More recently, this thinking has shifted. In fact, frozen fruit and vegetables can be just as nutritious — and fresh, sort of — as unfrozen. That's because a lot of companies snap freeze them, which means they are frozen almost the minute they have been pulled from the tree or vines. Special machinery is used to freeze at a temperature of -18°C, so that the nutrients are locked in and will stay potent for 3 to 6 months. Freezing herbs straight from the garden has the same effect. Or freeze the leftover herbs bought when the price is good. Herbs are not always in season and become more expensive the further they need to travel to the supermarket.

## HERBS TO FREEZE

BASIL: For pungent tomato sauces served over pasta and in lasagne.

CORIANDER: For fragrant Asian dressings and toppings.

THYME: For baking vegetables, meats and desserts with a savoury twist.

PARSLEY: For extra green and freshness in salads, sandwiches and soup toppings.

DILL: For an earthy flavour, great on potatoes or fish.

## HOW TO FREEZE

- Thoroughly wash the herbs and allow to dry. Use paper towels or, if there is a salad spinner in the cupboard that's even better.
- Remove leaves from the tough stems of herbs like rosemary and oregano.
- For herbs like coriander, parsley and dill, chop the herbs, stem and all, into chunks or flakes.
- If freezing whole leaves, place in a freezer bag to protect from directly hitting the ice.
- Put the herbs into ice cubes, fill with water and freeze. Store those herby cubes in a freezer bag and grab a handful as needed. Or soak the herbs in olive oil first and then freeze in ice cubes. The oil can help to preserve the full vibrant flavour.
- Frozen herbs will freeze well for up to 2 months.

## HOW TO DEFROST

- Defrost in the pan, as the sauce is simmering or the vegetables are sauteing. Otherwise, keep them in the fridge until cooking.
- Use within days of removing from the freezer.
- Avoid using hot water to defrost — the herbs will wilt almost instantly.

# Chicken Lasagne

A KID-FRIENDLY HOME-MADE DINNER THAT'S FANTASTIC TO HAVE IN THE FREEZER FOR THOSE BUSY MOMENTS LIFE BRINGS

**SERVES 4-6**

Oil, for frying

1 onion, finely chopped

1 clove garlic, chopped

2 carrots, peeled and diced

1 stalk celery, diced

1 cup (90g, 3oz) mushrooms, sliced

550g (1¼ lb) chicken mince

1 tbsp fresh or dried thyme (or oregano)

1 x 680g (24oz) bottle passata

Salt and pepper, to season

375g (13oz) lasagne sheets

¾ cup (90g, 3oz) mozzarella cheese, grated

**CHEESE SAUCE**

2 tbsps butter

2 tbsps plain flour

2 cups (500ml, 1pt) milk

½ cup (60g, 2oz) grated Parmesan cheese

Heat oil in a large saucepan over medium-high heat. Add onion and garlic and saute for 5 minutes, until soft and translucent. Add carrots and celery and cook, stirring, for 2-3 minutes until starting to soften, then add the mushrooms and cook for a further 3 minutes. Add chicken mince and herbs and cook, stirring, for 4-5 minutes until there is no sign of pink meat.

Pour in the passata and season with salt and pepper to taste. Stir to combine, then cover and allow to simmer for 15 minutes.

Pre-heat oven to 190°C (375°F, Gas Mark 5).

To make the cheese sauce, heat the butter in a saucepan over a low heat. Add the flour and mix until a smooth thick paste forms. Gradually add the milk and gently bring to the boil, stirring constantly. Add the Parmesan and stir through until melted.

Assemble in a medium-sized baking dish, starting with the meat sauce, then cheese sauce, then lasagna sheets. Repeat to form a second layer, making sure the lasagna is well covered, and finishing with the cheese sauce. Scatter the mozarella cheese over the top.

Cover loosely with foil and place in the oven to bake for 20 minutes. Remove foil, then return to the oven to bake for a further 5-10 minutes cheese is melted and golden brown.

# Fish Cakes

USE LEFTOVER SALMON TO MAKE THESE TASTY LITTLE FISHCAKES
AN EVEN BETTER BET FOR THE BUDGET - CONSCIOUS MUM

**SERVES 4**

4 medium potatoes,
peeled and chopped

1 x 225g (8oz) can
salmon

1 tbsp capers

1 tbsp flat-leaf parsley

Salt and pepper, to
season

2 eggs, beaten

½ cup (60g, 2oz)
breadcrumbs

1 tbsp olive oil

Lemon slices and
parsley, to serve

Place the potatoes in a large saucepan of salted water and bring
to the boil. Cook for 10 minutes, or until tender. Drain and
return to the pan. Roughly mash the potatoes using a potato
masher or fork. Place in a large bowl and allow to cool slighly.

Add the fish, capers and parsley to the bowl, and stir to combine.
Season with salt and pepper.

Gradually add about half the beaten egg to bring the mixture
together. The mixture should not be sloppy. Using your hands,
form mixture into patties.

Place the remaining egg in one bowl and breadcrumbs in
another. Dip each pattie into the egg, then breadcrumbs. If time
allows, transfer to the fridge for 30 minutes to firm up.

Heat the oil in a frying pan over a medium-high heat. Add the
fishcakes, and cook for 5 minutes on each side until golden and
crispy.

Serve with lemon slices and parsley garnish.

# Shepherd's Pie

WHEN ALL ELSE FAILS MAKE SHEPHERD'S PIE — THE ULTIMATE IN FILLING, COMFORTING FAMILY-FRIENDLY FARE

**SERVES 6**

1 tbsp olive oil

900g (2lb) lean beef mince

1 onion, chopped

3 cloves garlic, crushed

2 tbsps plain flour

¼ cup (30g, 1oz) instant gravy powder

2 cups (500ml, 1pt) beef stock or water

1 tbsp tomato paste

2 carrots, diced

1 cup (170g, 6oz) frozen peas

1 tbsp thyme leaves

4 large potatoes, chopped

50g (2oz) butter, chopped

½ cup (125ml, 4fl oz) milk

1 cup (125g, 4oz) Cheddar or mozarella cheese

Preheat the oven to 180°C (350°F, Gas Mark 4).

Heat oil in a frying pan over medium-high heat. Cook the mince in two batches for 8 minutes or until browned. Remove meat from pan. Add onion and garlic to pan and cook for 4-5 minutes until softened.

Return mince to pan and add flour. Cook, stirring, for 1 minute. Add gravy powder, stock, tomato paste and carrot and bring to the boil. Reduce heat to medium-low. Simmer, for 25-30 minutes, or until thickened, then add peas and thyme.

While meat is cooking, bring a saucepan of salted water to the boil and cook potatoes for 10 minutes or until tender. Drain.

Return drained potato to the pan over low heat and mash until smooth. Add butter and milk and stir until butter melts and mixture is combined.

Spoon mince into a casserole dish. Top with potato mixture and cheese. Transfer to the oven to bake for 25 minutes or until golden and bubbly.

# Broccoli Cheese Sticks

**SERVES 4**

2 cups (350g, 12oz) broccoli florets

1½ cups (130g, 4½ oz) rolled oats

1 spring onion, sliced

¼ cup (10g, ¼ oz) flat-leaf parsley

1 egg, beaten

1½ cups (185g, 6oz) cups Cheddar cheese, grated

Salt and pepper, to taste

Preheat the oven to 200°C (400°F, Gas Mark 6). Line a large baking tray with baking paper and set aside.

Cook the broccoli in boiling water for 2 minutes then remove and run under cold water in a colander.

In a food processer, pulse the broccoli, oats, spring onions and parsley until you have a finely chopped mix. Place broccoli mixture in a large bowl and mix through the egg, cheese, salt and pepper.

Scoop small handfuls of mix and shape into logs using your hands. Place on the baking tray. Bake for 20 minutes until golden brown and crispy, flipping them over half way. Remove from the oven and enjoy hot with your favourite condiment.

# Meatballs in Tomato Sauce

**SERVES 6-8**

6 tomatoes, chopped

2 tsps fennel seeds

3 cups (750ml, 24fl oz) passata

Salt and pepper, to taste

1kg (2lb) beef mince

2 eggs

¾ cup (90g, 3oz) breadcrumbs

1 clove garlic, minced

¼ cup (30g, 1oz) Parmesan cheese, grated

Fresh parsley, to garnish

Fry chopped tomatoes and fennel seeds in a large frying pan over a medium-high heat for 5 minutes or until soft. Add passata, salt and pepper and stir to combine. Reduce heat to low and cover.

Combine beef, eggs, breadcrumbs, garlic, salt and Parmesan in a large bowl.

Using your hands shape into meatballs of a roughly equal size. Place the meatballs into simmering sauce, cover and cook for 35 minutes, or until meat is cooked through. Serve garnished with parsley.

# TOMATO SAUCE ON HAND

Dinner time in a family of three, four or more is energetic, perhaps mildly chaotic — and of course fun. It's a simple bit of genius to have ready-made healthy sauces for evenings when there's only time or supplies to empty a packet of noodles into boiling water. Tomato sauce is pumping with vitamins and antioxidants and can be eaten as soup if nothing else. Adding basil, grated cheese, avocado, olives — whatever is in the crisper — is all bonus goodness and novelty. Tomato sauce easily freezes and can defrost through the school day or with a nudge from boiling water.

# Spinach Lasagne

## LASAGNA IS ALWAYS A WINNER AND THIS RECIPE'S A CINCH — A GREAT OPTION FOR MEAT-FREE MONDAYS

**SERVES 6**

2 bunches of spinach, or 300g (10oz) frozen spinach)

2 cups (450g, 1lb) cottage cheese (or ricotta)

2 cups (250g, 8oz) mozzarella cheese, divided

1 egg

1 tsp salt

¼ tsp black pepper

1 tsp oregano, ground

1 x 500g (1lb 2oz) jar passata

9 lasagne sheets

Preheat the oven to 180°C (350°F, Gas Mark 4).

If using fresh spinach, rinse, drain and pat dry. If using frozen, ensure it is thawed before proceeding.

In a large bowl combine the spinach, cottage cheese (or ricotta), half of the mozzarella, egg, salt and pepper and oregano.

Lightly oil a large, deep-sided oven dish. Start by adding a layer of sauce, using a third of the jar. Then add lasagna, using as many sheets as needed to fill the dish in a single layer. Add spinach-cheese mixture next, and then repeat the layering finishing with sauce. Sprinkle the remaining mozzarella on top of this final layer.

Transfer to the oven to bake for 1 hour. Check after 45 minutes and if the top is browning too much cover with foil and return to the oven for the last 15 minutes.

Remove from the oven and set aside to cool slightly for 15 minutes before serving.

# Beetroot Burgers

THESE VERSATILE BURGER PATTIES CAN BE GLUTEN FREE, OR NOT, AND SERVED LIGHT ON PITAS OR IN BURGER BUNS WITH THE WORKS

**SERVES 6**

2 medium-sized beetroots

1 tbsp olive oil

1 onion, finely chopped

1 clove garlic, minced

½ tsp ground cumin

2 cups (400g, 14oz) cooked lentils

1 cup (190g, 7oz) cooked quinoa (or breadcrumbs)

½ cup (60g, 2oz) buckwheat flour (or plain flour)

1 egg

½ lemon, juiced

Salt and pepper, to taste

Wholemeal pita bread or burger buns, to serve

Preheat oven to 190°C (375°F, Gas Mark 5). Brush a baking tray with oil and line with baking paper.

Peel the beetroots using a knife or potato peeler and grate them using a box grater. Set aside.

Heat the olive oil in a frying pan over a medium heat. Add the onion and cook for 5 minutes until soft and starting to caramelise. Add the garlic and cook for a further minute or so until soft and fragrant. Add the cumin and cook for a further minute. Remove the pan from the heat and set aside.

Place the lentils in a food processor and pulse until roughly ground, but not so much as to form a paste.

Transfer the lentils to a large mixing bowl. Add the quinoa (or breadcrumbs), flour, egg and grated beetroot and stir to combine. Add the onion and lemon juice. Season to taste with salt and pepper. At this stage, check for consistency of the mixture which should stick together well. If it doesn't, add more flour.

Using your hands, shape into patties of desired size. Place burger patties on the prepared baking tray and transfer to the oven to bake for 35 minutes. Flip the patties once during this time.

Remove and allow to cool slightly. Serve with wholemeal pita bread or burger buns.

Let's Party

# Princess Cupcakes

SWEET AND SIMPLE MINI CUPCAKES, PERFECT FOR A LITTLE GIRL'S
BIRTHDAY PARTY OR AFTERNOON TEA

**MAKES 24**

### CUPCAKES

150g (5oz) butter,
room temperature

1½ cups (330g, 12oz)
caster sugar

2 eggs

2½ cups (310g, 10oz)
self-raising flour

1¼ cups (310ml, 10fl
oz) milk

2 tsps vanilla essence

### ICING

100g (3½ oz) butter,
room temperature

1½ cups (235g, 8oz)
icing sugar

2 drops vanilla essence

2 tbsps milk

Pink and yellow food
colouring

Rainbow pearls, to
decorate

Preheat the oven to 190°C (375°F, Gas Mark 5). Place paper cases in a mini muffin tray.

Using an electric mixer, beat butter until smooth, add caster sugar and beat well until light and fluffy. Add eggs and beat. Add the sifted flour, milk and vanilla and stir until a smooth batter forms. Spoon mixture into the cases to about a third full.

Bake for 20 minutes until golden or until springy to touch. Turn out onto a wire rack to cool while you prepare the icing.

In an electric mixer, beat butter until it is pale and fluffy. Sift over the icing sugar and add the vanilla essence and milk. Beat until the mixture has a light, fluffy texture. Add extra milk for a softer consistency. Add drops of food colouring, 1 drop at a time to achieve the desired colour. Spread or pipe icing over cupcakes and top with decorations as desired.

# Gingerbread Imagination Cookies

CREATE GINGERBREAD MEN, WOMEN, CIRCLES, STARS OR WHATEVER SHAPE YOU LIKE — A FUN ACTIVITY FOR A RAINY AFTERNOON WITH THE KIDS

**MAKES 30**

125g (4oz) butter, room temperature

²/₃ cup (100g, 3oz) brown sugar

¼ cup (60ml, 2fl oz) maple syrup

1 egg, lightly beaten

2½ cups (310g, 10oz) plain flour

½ tsp bicarbonate of soda

1 tbsp ground ginger

2 tsps ground cinnamon

Preheat oven to 180°C (350°F, Gas Mark 4). Line three baking trays with greaseproof paper.

Using an electric mixer, beat butter and sugar until light and fluffy. Add maple syrup and egg and beat to combine.

Sift flour, bicarb, ginger and cinnamon over butter mixture. Stir until just combined and a soft dough forms.

Place dough on a floured surface and knead gently until smooth. Shape the dough into a disk and wrap in plastic wrap. Refrigerate for 1 hour.

Roll dough out to a thickness of 5mm (¼ in). Cut shapes from dough using cookie cutters. Place on baking trays about 2cm (1in) apart.

Bake one tray at a time for 20 minutes, or until firm to touch. Stand on trays for 5 minutes, before transferring to a wire rack to cool completely.

# Homemade Ice-Cream Sandwiches

YOU'LL BE SUPER-MUM FOR SURE WHEN YOU SERVE UP THIS SWEET, COOL AND CRUNCHY TREAT AT YOUR KIDS' PARTY

**SERVES 6**

150g (5½ oz) butter, room temperature

½ cup (100g, 3½ oz) caster sugar

½ cup (80g, 3oz) packed brown sugar

1 tsp vanilla extract

1 egg

1¾ cups (215g, 7oz) plain flour

½ cup (85g, 3oz) dark chocolate chips

½ cup (85g, 3oz) milk chocolate chips

1 tub chocolate chip ice cream

Preheat oven to 180°C (350°F, Gas Mark 4) and line two baking trays with greaseproof paper.

Place butter, sugars and vanilla in an electric mixer and beat for 1-2 minutes until smooth and well combined. Add egg and whisk until combined.

Add the flour in two batches, stirring after each addition. Add the dark and milk choc chips and mix thoroughly.

Measure level tablespoons, rolling into balls and placing on prepared trays approximately 3cm (1in) apart. Press down slightly on each ball.

Bake for 15 minutes or until golden. When cooked, remove from the oven and transfer to a wire rack to cool.

To assemble, spoon ice cream onto one cookie and sandwich with another. Use a knife to smooth the edges around the ice cream.

# Chocolate Popcorn

**SERVES 4**

400g (14oz) milk or dark chocolate, broken into pieces

30g (1oz) butter

2 tsp vanilla extract

8 tbsps water

6 cups (65g, 2oz) freshly popped popcorn

Preheat the oven to 110°C (230°F, Gas Mark ¼). Line a baking tray with greaseproof paper.

Melt the chocolate, butter, vanilla and water in a heatproof bowl over a pan of boiling water. Stir constantly until the chocolate is smooth and shiny.

Place popcorn in a large bowl. Working quickly, immediately pour the chocolate sauce over the top of the popcorn and stir until it's evenly coated with the sauce.

Spread out the popcorn over the tray in a single layer. Bake in the oven for 30 minutes. Remove the mixture and stir, then bake for another 30 minutes. Remove from oven and let the popcorn cool. Break apart and store in an airtight container.

# Caramel Popcorn

**SERVES 4**

225g (8oz) unsalted butter

2 cups (440g, 1lb) brown sugar

½ cup (180g, 6oz) honey

1 tsp salt

½ tsp bicarbonate of soda

1 tsp vanilla extract

6 cups (65g, 2oz) freshly popped popcorn

Preheat oven to 110°C (230°F, Gas Mark ¼). Line a large tray with baking paper.

Melt butter in saucepan over medium heat. Stir in brown sugar, honey and salt. Keep stirring and bring to the boil for 5 minutes, stirring frequently. Remove from heat and mix through the bicarb and vanilla. The mixture will bubble and then reduce in size.

Place popcorn in a large bowl. Working quickly, pour the caramel sauce over the popcorn and stir until evenly coated with the sauce. Spread out the popcorn over the tray in a single layer. Bake in the oven for 30 minutes. Remove the mixture and stir, then bake for another 30 minutes. Remove from oven and let the popcorn cool. Break apart and store in an airtight container.

# CAKE POPS

In fantasy lands where there are fairies and goblins and dragons and dragonflies living together, there are also cake pops. Surely, a child with a big imagination invented these: a lollipop made of cake. They might be eaten for breakfast, lunch and dinner in this imaginary place. In reality, they are probably best for special occasions. Baking, icing and decorating cake pops makes for a dreamy rainy day in the kitchen. And an excellent challenge for the kids: come up with their healthiest cake pop ideas. And then go wild creating them.

## BAKE A CAKE POP

- Bake a cake and cool it on a rack.
- Break the cake up in a big bowl and get all the little hands in there to help.
- Add icing for moisture — firm, not runny. Create a dough that can be rolled into balls.
- The fun part: roll the cake dough into perfect balls (or perfectly fantastical ball-like shapes — perfection is not essential).
- Place balls on a tray lined with baking paper, then stick the tray in the fridge or freezer.

## DO THE DIP

The classic coating for a cake pop is … chocolate! Use dark, milk, white or even flavoured chocolate.

Cooking chocolate is best for melting. Once the little ones have stuck each cake ball with a lollipop stick, then comes the swirl. Hold the cake pops firmly and dip in melted chocolate, covering as evenly as possible. Then to the fridge or freezer again.

## EXPERIMENT WITH HEALTHY OPTIONS

- Mix white flour with almond flour, whole wheat flour, quinoa flour or spelt flour. for greater nutrient, fibre and protein content.
- Try almond or coconut milks in the icing, rather than full cream milk.
- Add beetroot to cake mixture for extra moisture and vitamin C.
- Carrot and fruit cakes are as delicious and more nutritious than classic chocolate or vanilla cake.

## TOPPINGS

Lay out little bowls for a decorating party. Add sprinkles before the chocolate coating has set. For the healthiest pops that still taste magical use:
- Finely chopped strawberries
- Almonds or walnuts, flaked or crumbled
- Coconut, flaked or desiccated (rub with a bit of food colouring for a healthy 'sprinkle')
- Good ol' sprinkles, a treat that kids love.

# Chocolate Fudge and White Chocolate Cake Pops

THESE FUN-PACKED BITE-SIZED MORSELS ARE A HIT FOR KIDS' PARTIES AND YOU — OR THEY — CAN DECORATE THEM TO SUIT

**SERVES 24**

1 chocolate fudge cake

225g (8oz, ½ lb) cream cheese, room temperature

4 tbsps butter

2 cups (310g, 10oz) icing sugar

1 tbsp milk (or more, as necessary)

Cake pop or lollipop sticks

700g (1½ lb) white chocolate chips

Coloured sugars, candies, and other decorative sprinkles

Break the cake into a large bowl and crumble with fingers or a fork to a breadcrumb consistency.

In a separate bowl, whip the cream cheese, butter, icing sugar and milk together until smooth. Scrape into the bowl with the cake crumbs and mix with with fingers until fully incorporated. Add additional milk, as required, until the mixture will hold together when rolled into a ball.

Roll all the mixture into balls and insert sticks. Place in the freezer for about 20 minutes.

When ready to prepare the cake pops, melt the chocolate. Place chocolate in a heatproof bowl over a pan of simmering water on a medium heat (or melt chocolate in microwave).

Prepare decorations by sprinkling them onto pieces of greaseproof paper.

Dip the cake pops into the chocolate and fully submerge.

Let the excess chocolate drip off. Swirl and tap gently if needed.

Roll the cake pops in sprinkles and other decorations as desired.

# AVOCADOS

These beautiful green fruits are close to a miracle food. Avocados have helped define the term 'good fat' for many a home chef feeding young ones or children of several ages. There's no other food in the fruit bowl that can be described as 'rich and fatty' and yet we are advised to it eat pretty much every day — it's the ice cream of the fruit world. (One avocado contains about 25-30g of fat; mostly of the monounsaturated variety, which for big and little hearts is like taking a quick shower, then lathering on the moisturiser.) Avocados are a healthy habit and make meal planning a bit easier.

The fat is what makes them creamy, which makes them amazing for salad dressings and dips. The ideal seasonings are light and acidic condiments like lime juice, coriander, lemon, red onions, vinegar and chilli. They're also brilliant in all sorts of desserts, especially ice cream and mousses — they add creaminess and mellow out overly sugary dishes.

Most days, avocados can be enjoyed in their pure state: soaked in lemon and pepper and scooped straight from the skin. Dollop on some cottage cheese for extra protein. Or give an avocado to a toddler and watch the many messy, delightful ways it can be scooped and gorged on — it might give ideas for new dishes.

## IDEAS FOR INCLUDING AVOCADO

GRILLED AVOCADOS: Drizzle in oil, then lay the flat surface of a half avocado across the heated grill or barbecue for just a few minutes. The grill will sear crunchy, bronze strips into the creamy flesh and the average avocado will become a little chewy on top, airy in the middle and come to life with the oily, salty flavour of charring.

PERFECTLY WHIPPED GUACAMOLE: There are a lot of variations of guacamole, though this citrusy dip barely needs a thing but avocados, lime, maybe salt and pepper, or onion and chilli if you like. Use avocados that ripened today or even yesterday to ensure it doesn't go mushy yet is soft enough to scoop with a carrot stick. Just be sure to slice off brown bits that can get stringy.

AVOCADO ON TOAST: Otherwise known as 'avocado smash' and served in popular cafes and even gourmet restaurants all over the world. What a simple delight. Mash it up, spread it on seeded breads, then add all sorts of toppings — feta and ricotta cheese, sun-dried tomatoes and chives, a perfectly fried egg and hot sauce (or tomato sauce for less adventurous taste buds …).

# Chocolate Avocado Muffins

THE AVOCADO IS DEFINITELY HIDING IN THESE MOIST AND CHOCOLATEY MUFFINS; LEAVE OFF THE ICING FOR A LOW-SUGAR VERSION

**MAKES 12**

1½ cups (185g, 6oz) whole wheat flour

½ cup (60g, 2oz) cocoa powder

1 tsp baking powder

¾ tsp bicarbonate of soda

½ tsp salt

1 ripe avocado, peeled and seeded

½ cup (180g, 6oz) maple syrup

¾ cup (185ml, 6fl oz) almond milk

⅓ cup (80ml, 3fl oz) olive oil or coconut oil, melted

1 tsp vanilla

⅓ cup (60g, 2oz) mini dark chocolate chips

**ICING**

220g (8oz) dark chocolate, chopped

230g (8oz) butter, room temperature, chopped

1½ tbsps milk

1 cup (170g, 6oz) icing sugar

Preheat oven to 180°C (350°F, Gas Mark 4). Line a 12-hole muffin tray and fill with muffin liners.

Combine the flour, cocoa, baking powder, bicarb and salt. Set aside. In a food processor, blend the avocado with the maple syrup, almond milk, oil and vanilla.

Add the wet ingredients to the dry ingredients and stir until combined and all ingredients are wet. Stir in the chocolate chips.

Spoon the mixture into the prepared tins.

Place in the oven and bake for 15 minutes or until a skewer inserted into the centre comes out clean. Stand in tray for 5 minutes. Transfer to a wire rack to cool.

To make the icing, melt chocolate in a small heatproof bowl over a simmering saucepan of water.

Using an electric mixer, beat butter until creamy. Add milk and beat until mixed. Add chocolate and beat until fully incorporated. Add icing sugar and beat until creamy.

Spread, or pipe, icing onto cool muffins.

# Avocado Lime Cheesecake

ZESTY, CREAMY AND A HEALTHIER CHOICE THAN MOST, THIS NO-BAKE CHEESECAKE WILL SUPRISE AND DELIGHT

**SERVES 8-10**

**CRUST**

2½ cups (310g, 10oz) macadamia nuts

½ cup (40g, 1½ oz) desiccated coconut

6 dates

2 tbsps cacao powder

2 tbsps coconut oil

**FILLING**

5 avocados, peeled and seeded

1 cup (250ml, 8fl oz) lime juice

2 limes, zested (reserve some for garnish)

1 cup (250g, 9oz) coconut yoghurt

1 tsp vanilla extract

¾ cup (165g, 6oz) caster sugar

2 tbsps gelatin powder

Cream or coconut yoghurt, to decorate

Prepare a round and high springform tin with baking paper.

Place the crust ingredients into a high-speed blender or food processor and process until combined and a sticky dough has formed.

Scrape mixture into the centre of the prepared tin and push evenly and firmly over the base to create a smooth and even finish. Transfer to the fridge to chill while you complete the next steps.

To make the filling, place all the ingredients except the gelatin and cream in a food processor and blend until smooth. Taste the mixture and add more sugar, lime or vanilla according to taste.

Mix gelatin powder with 2 tablespoons of cold water and set aside for a couple of minutes, then add 3 tablespoons of boiling water. Stir well to ensure it is smooth then add to the food processor and blend again until very smooth.

Remove cake tin from fridge and pour filling over the base. Cover with a plate or plastic wrap, and return to the fridge to set for at least 4-5 hours or overnight.

Decorate with lime zest and cream or coconut yoghurt to serve.

**NOTE:** This cheesecake is great frozen. Simply cover in plastic wrap and remove an hour before you'd like to serve it.

# Avocado Smoothie Pops

**SERVES 4**

1 avocado, peeled and seeded

1 banana, sliced

1½ cups (375ml, 13fl oz) milk

2 tsps honey

½ cup (75g, 3oz) ice cubes

Add all the ingredients to the blender and process until smooth.

Pour evenly into icy-pole moulds, insert sticks and place in the freezer for at least 1 hour to set.

# Mint Choc Chip Blocks

**MAKES 6**

1½ tsps peppermint extract

2-4 drops green food colouring

2½ cups (625ml, 20fl oz) milk

2 bananas, sliced

1 cup (175g, 6oz) dark chocolate chips

1 tbsp honey

Add all the ingredients to the blender and process until smooth.

Pour evenly into icy-pole moulds, insert sticks and place in the freezer for at least 1 hour to set.

# HOME – MADE ICE CREAM

It has to be the ultimate treat: ice cream that the kids make themselves … with a little help from a parent and ideally an ice-cream maker, which is an excellent investment for dessert-loving households. A food processor or blender also does the job, just with a little extra fiddling. Also needed: cream, eggs, milk, sugar, vanilla extract and a pinch of salt. That's it for the basic bowl of vanilla deliciousness. Then add anything — strawberries, cherries, cacao nibs, pumpkin, honey, chocolate biscuits. Sorbets can also be made in the ice-cream maker for the fruitier versions of this timeless, magical treat.

# MAKE YOUR OWN BREAD AND NUT CRUMBS

Fish fingers, fish 'n' chips, chicken fingers, chicken nuggets, chicken wings, fried zucchini, stuffed mushrooms. They're all fun food that have one thing in common: they're breaded or battered, which is delicious but not super healthy, especially eaten regularly. Making flours and breading at home can turn a naughty treat into a nutritional treat that works great for dinners and school snacks.

## NUT CRUMBS

The only ingredients in most nut crumbs: nuts and perhaps salt and pepper. Throw a big bag of almonds, hazelnuts or sesame seeds into the food processor and blend them until they are as fine as flour (but watch out they don't turn into butter!) Dip fish, chicken, pork or vegetables into egg before lathering in the fine flour that is now bursting with omega-3s and antioxidants.

Be aware that delicate nut flours burn at lower temperatures than grain-based flours, which means the crumb might cook before the vegetables or meats. To counter this, mix nut flours with whole wheat, white or spelt flours. Store-bought almond flour is often organic and perfectly delicious for battering fillets of white fish or slices of eggplant. Add Parmesan cheese for a creamy and slightly lemony flavour.

## BREADCRUMBS

For a batch of classic breadcrumbs, take a loaf of white bread — this is a great solution for the bread that the kids haven't devoured — soak in olive oil and stick in the oven or grill to turn into crunchy toast. Break the toast into chunks, then blend into finer chunks or a fine powder as desired.

Of course, things can get a lot more nutritious and inventive. Sourdough bread has a zesty, somewhat buttery flavour. Buy sourdough croutons already made or start from scratch and pick up a fresh loaf from the bakery and make the croutons at home. Keep a few pieces for toast and marmalade, then cut the rest into cubes and bake for 10 minutes at 300°C. Let cool for 10 minutes, then throw them in the food processor and season with salt and pepper. Or try whole wheat bread with oregano — the herb is fragrant and absorbs beautifully into the nutty, earthy bread. Turn the bread into well-baked toast and process until all the chunks are smooth or very fine.

## SAVE CRUMBS FOR LATER

For nut and breadcrumbs, store in airtight containers for a few days, or freeze for meals up to 3 months down the track.

# Almond-Crusted Chicken Nuggets

JUICY, CRUNCHY, DELICIOUS CHICKEN NUGGETS WITH NONE OF THE NASTIES
OF PRE-MADE VERSIONS — FREEZE LEFTOVERS FOR AN EASY SNACK

**SERVES 4**

1¼ cups (150g, 5oz) almond meal

1 tbsp paprika

1 tsp cayenne pepper

1 tsp salt

1 tsp black pepper

2 eggs

3 chicken breasts, cut into bite-sized chunks

¼ cup (60g, 2oz) tomato sauce, for dipping

Preheat the oven to 235°C (455°F, Gas Mark 8). Grease and line a baking tray.

Mix the almond meal, spices and salt and pepper in a bowl and transfer the mixture to a flat plate.

In a separate bowl, whisk together the eggs.

Next, create your nuggets. Take one or two chicken pieces and cover in plastic wrap. Gently pound with a meat tenderiser or rolling pin to the desired thickness. Repeat until all chicken is prepared.

Dip chicken into eggs, then dip into almond mixture, fully coating. Repeat with all chicken pieces.

Place coated chicken pieces on the baking tray.

Bake for 30 minutes, turning after 15 minutes, until golden.

Serve with tomato sauce for dipping.

# Lamb and Mushroom Pasties

## THESE POPULAR LITTLE PARTY SNACKS ARE SIMPLE, AFFORDABLE AND TASTY

**MAKES 18**

1 tsp olive oil

6 spring onions, sliced

½ tsp ground cumin

½ tsp ground coriander

600g (1lb 5oz) lamb mince

12 button mushrooms, finely diced

6 sheets frozen puff pastry, thawed

2 eggs, beaten

2 tbsps sesame seeds (white and black)

Preheat the oven to 200°C (400°F, Gas Mark 6) and line two large baking trays with baking paper.

Heat oil in a frying pan over medium-high heat. Add spring onions and cook, stirring, for 3 minutes until soft. Add cumin and coriander and cook for a further 1 minute, stirring, until aromatic.

Add mince and cook, stirring to break up lumps, for a further 5 minutes until browned.

Add mushrooms and cook for a further 4 minutes until mushrooms are tender and any liquid from the meat and mushroom has evaporated.

Cut each pastry sheet into four circles. Place 2 heaped tablespoons of mince mixture at the centre of each.

Brush around the perimeter of the pastry circle with a little of the beaten egg, then fold the pastry over the mixture. Starting at one side, crimp the edges over to form a seal.

Place pasties on prepared trays and brush with remaining egg. Sprinkle with sesame seeds, then transfer to the oven and bake for 10 minutes or until golden.

# Upside Down Muffins

THE QUIRKY TWIST OF TURNING THESE TASTY MUFFINS UPSIDE DOWN
WILL INTRIGUE AND DELIGHT LITTLE PEOPLE

**MAKES 12**

1½ cups (185g, 6oz)
plain flour

2 tsps baking powder

2 zucchinis, grated

1 sweet potato, peeled
and grated

½ cup (80g, 3oz)
sun-dried tomatoes,
chopped

⅓ cup (40g, 1½ oz)
Parmesan cheese,
finely grated

2 eggs

⅓ cup (80ml, 3fl oz)
milk

2 tbsps olive oil

Basil leaves, to garnish

Preheat oven to 180°C (350°F, Gas Mark 4) and grease and line a
12-hole muffin tray with paper cases.

Sift flour and baking powder over a large bowl. Add zucchini,
sweet potato, sun-dried tomatoes and Parmesan cheese.

Whisk together eggs, milk and oil in a separate bowl.

Add wet ingredients to dry ingredients and stir until just
combined, being careful not to over-mix. Spoon mixture into
muffin tray to two-thirds of the way full.

Bake for 20 minutes or until golden in colour and a skewer
inserted into the centre comes out clean.

Place on a wire rack to cool. When cool, carefully remove paper
cases and serve upside down.

# Mini Cheeseburgers

KIDS AND ADULTS LOVE THE NOVELTY OF THESE - SERVE THEM AT A PARTY AND SEE HAPPY FACES GOBBLE THEM UP

**MAKES 8**

12 small dinner rolls

1 egg, beaten

1 tsp water

1 tbsp sesame seeds

½ cup (60g, 2oz) seasoned breadcrumbs

2 eggs, lightly beaten

1½ tsps Worcestershire sauce

3 spring onions, finely chopped

1 clove garlic, crushed

500g (1lb 2oz) beef mince

6 long rashers bacon, halved

3 slices tasty cheese, quartered

6 leaves of butter lettuce, halved

3 Roma tomatoes, sliced

12 small wooden skewers

Slice each roll in half. Mix egg and water together in a small bowl and brush over tops of rolls. Sprinkle with sesame seeds. Bake at 165°C (330°F, Gas Mark 3) for 10 minutes. Remove from oven and let the rolls cool.

In a large bowl, combine the breadcrumbs, egg, Worcestershire sauce, spring onions, garlic and beef. Using your hands, shape into 12 patties.

Heat a grill pan over high heat. Place the meat patties on the grill and cook for 3 minutes on each side or until cooked through. Remove from the grill and place the cheese quarters on the burgers straight away. At the same time, heat a frying pan on high heat and fry the bacon rashers for 2 minutes on each side or until cooked how you like it.

To assemble each burger layer on the bottom half of each bun a lettuce leaf, cheese-covered patty, tomato slice, and top half of the bun. Hold burgers together with the wooden skewers through the centre of each bun.

# Garden Cupcakes

**MAKES 12**

1¾ cups (215g, 7oz) self-raising flour

1 tbsp cocoa

1 cup (220g, 8oz) caster sugar

125g (4oz) butter, room temperature, chopped

2 eggs

½ cup (125ml, 4fl oz) milk

1 tsp vanilla extract

10 drops green food colouring

Buttercream frosting (see recipe page 298)

Marzipan flowers

Preheat oven to 190°C (375°F, Gas Mark 5). Line a 12-hole muffin pan with paper cases. Sift flour and cocoa in the bowl of an electric mixer. Add sugar, butter, eggs, milk and vanilla and beat on medium-low for 5 minutes, until pale and creamy. Spoon into muffin cups. Bake for 20 minutes or until a skewer comes out clean. Cool on a wire rack. Mix green food colouring with the buttercream. Pipe icing onto cupcakes in thin strips. Pull up and away when icing strand is long enough, about 1cm (½ in). For a wavy effect, occasionally pull tip slightly to one side. Keep grass clusters close together to cover cake. Top with marzipan flowers.

# Butterfly Puffs

**MAKES 14**

4 puff pastry sheets

400g (14oz) frozen blueberries

2 tbsps icing sugar

Preheat the oven to 180°C (350°F, Gas Mark 4).

Place your puff pastry sheets on baking paper and cut out 4 butterflies per sheet using a cookie cutter or paper template. Arrange the butterflies on the baking paper. Use leftover scraps of pastry to create antennae or to decorate the wings further if you feel like.

Press the frozen blueberries gently into each butterfly.

Bake your puffs for 15 minutes or until the pastry has turned golden brown.

Sprinkle with icing sugar.

# Spider Eggs

HOSTING HALLOWEEN THIS YEAR? HERE'S A HEALTHY AND EASY OPTION THAT'LL SCARE THE TASTEBUDS OFF THE NEIGHBOURHOOD

**MAKES 12**

6 eggs, hard boiled and peeled

¼ cup (60ml, 2fl oz) mayonnaise

1 tsp Dijon or American mustard

¼ tsp of salt

Pinch of smoked paprika

12 pitted black olives

Salt and pepper, to taste

Slice the boiled eggs in half. Gently scoop out the yolks and place in a small mixing bowl.

Mash the yolks and then stir in mayonnaise, mustard, salt and paprika until well blended. Mash and stir all ingredients together well. Season further to taste with salt and pepper.

Spoon a little bit of the mixture into each egg white half, ensuring it's equally divided.

Slice the pitted black olives in half lengthwise and sit a half on top of the yolk mixture in each egg to make the spiders' bodies. Then slice the other olive halves crossways and then in half again. Place these on top of the egg yolks around the spider to form the legs.

Sprinkle extra paprika over the eggs and serve.

# Little Cucumber People

FUN, EASY AND ADORABLE — THESE HEALTHY SNACKS WILL GO DOWN A TREAT AT ANY GET-TOGETHER WHERE KIDS ARE INVOLVED

**MAKES 12**

16 bowtie pasta shapes (plus extra shapes to allow for any breakages)

Pinch of salt

1 continental cucumber

24 currants

1-2 radishes

6 chives, 4 finely chopped and 2 sliced lengthways

250g (9oz) cream cheese, softened

6 slices pumpernickel bread

Thyme, roughly chopped

Bring some water to a boil in a medium-sized pot. Add pasta and a pinch of salt. Cook pasta according to package directions. Allow to cool.

Use a small scorer to score vertical lines down the length of the cucumber, about 1cm (½ in) apart. Slice the cucumber into 12 even slices and push two currents into the top quarter of each, to make the eyes. Set aside. Thinly slice radishes crossways and cut each circle in half.

Mix together the chopped chives with cream cheese in a bowl.

With a small biscuit or scone cutter, cut two circles out of each slice of pumpernickel and set on a serving plate. Spoon a heaped teaspoon of the cream cheese mixture onto each circle of bread. Place each piece of cucumber upright towards the back of the cream cheese. Place a piece of radish on the cucumber slice for the mouth.

Wrap each bowtie in a slice of chive and place in front of the cucumber, upright. Sprinkle with thyme to taste.

# Halloween Witches' Hats

## A SPOOKY TREAT THAT MIGHT JUST BE AS MUCH FUN TO MAKE AS IT IS TO EAT

**SERVES 10**

**BUTTERCREAM FROSTING**

125g (4oz) butter, room temperature

1½ cups (235g, 8oz) icing sugar mixture

1 tbsp milk

Blue and red food colouring

**WITCHES' HAT CONES**

5 tsps polka dot cake decorations, or sprinkles

10 dark waffle ice cream cones

10 Marie biscuits

1 small pineapple, peeled, cored and chopped into small pieces

First make the frosting. Using an electric mixer, beat the butter in a bowl until soft and pale. Gradually add icing sugar mixture and milk, beating constantly until combined. Add more milk if needed. Add blue and red colour drop by drop to the frosting to obtain desired shade. Stir well.

Next, assemble your witches' hats. Enlist the help of the kids at this stage for a fun activity!

Spread the frosting out on a clean plate or work surface. Sprinkle the sprinkles on a separate plate. Take a cone and dunk the end of it in the frosting. Roll the dunked end in the sprinkles to create a nice coating of sprinkles for the base of the hat.

Put a dollop of frosting onto each of the 10 Marie biscuits and set aside.

Next, fill the cones with chopped pineapple.

Place a Marie biscuit on the top of each cone and turn it upside down so the biscuit is on the base and transfer to a serving plate.

Put a dot of icing on the tip of each witches' hat and sprinkle with polka dots.

**NOTE:** Switch the pineapple for Halloween-themed lollies for an extra fun treat for the kids.